Tea on the Way North

Rosie Elizabeth Clifton

DEDICATION

For Nan, until we meet again.

CONTENTS

JOHN O'GROATS

NORTH SEA

CAIRNGORMS NATIONAL PARK

GLASGOW

EDINBURGH

LAKE DISTRICT

IRISH SEA

LEEDS

LIVERPOOL

SHEFFIELD

WALES

BIRMINGHAM (HOME)

LONDON

1

BEGINNINGS

It's been more than 18 months since the world descended into chaos following the spread of COVID-19. We're now used to the rules that have governed life lately, and we can begin to think about life beyond social distancing and having to remember what zone level we live in. It is at this point, in October 2022, that we finally start to plan a route for our long-time-planned Scotland trip and when – of course – our van starts to show signs of weakness. Vera – the name originating from the first two letters of the number plate, VE, and seeming to suit her sturdy, mature personality well – has been our four-wheeled companion for five years. However, the brakes are going, one brake light doesn't work due to an electrical fault, the driver-side door lock has a mind of its own, there have been issues starting the engine a couple of times and that constantly squeaking clutch pedal refuses to give us a break.

But we have to do the trip in Vera. That's always been the plan. While

James has been building our campervan-in-a-box solution, we've been dreaming of waking up in the Scottish highlands with the back doors open and a wild, green landscape as our view.

On a cold November day, after managing most of a day's window cleaning jobs, James slowly limps Vera home and drives her straight into the garage next door, only to discover that the clutch is almost at the point of exploding through the bonnet. Mechanic Steve tells us in no uncertain terms that we cannot drive another inch. Five hundred pounds later and a new clutch, Vera's got a new lease of life. Our bank accounts are looking a little worse for wear, though. Still, we're excited to know that Vera will still be the vehicle to ferry us around Scotland for two weeks.

We bought Vera, a 2009-plate Citroen Berlingo multi-space, in 2018. She was sold to us as a solid, basic sort of van, without the bells and whistles of air con and electric windows, but a car that would last a long time. She's not disappointed. Sure, on hot summer days, the lack of air con makes it feel like you're driving a microwave, and scraping thick ice from the windscreen has taken a few minutes out of some winter workdays. But all in all, Vera's carried us to Cornwall, Norfolk, the Lakes and now – hopefully – the far reaches of Scotland.

The idea of transforming our little van into a temporary campervan was brought about, initially, by the discovery of a handwritten note on a scrap of paper in my Nan's former bedroom.

My wonderful Nan, Doreen Cecilia Banks nee Gunn, passed away in April 2020 during one of the strangest periods of the pandemic. She lived with my Mom around the corner from James and me. Until James and I got married in 2017, it had been me, Mom and Nan for 22 years. My Nan could be a strong-willed woman, but mostly she was warm, gentle and generous. She was a resilient woman, too, enduring for many years despite a broken hip, several mini-strokes and various other illnesses.

Growing up, I don't think I really appreciated the special relationship I had with Nan; it seemed the most normal thing in the world to live with my Nan. However, and especially since her death, I've come to realise the privilege it was to have been, in part, raised by her. She spoiled me rotten while also tirelessly trying to train me to be more ladylike as well as to teach me how to speak properly – always emphasising the 'T's in 'isn't it' every time I omitted their pronunciation. Nan loved all her children, grandchildren and great grandchildren, but what a blessing to have spent so much time with her.

I moved back in with Mom and Nan briefly that April, when things weren't looking too good. Mom and I took turns to sit with her through the night in the few days before she finally went to sleep peacefully on the morning of April 16th, with her left hand in Mom's and her right in mine. Nan was always an elegant, dignified lady, and she slipped away in a very dignified and calm manner. Very Nan. I was glad.

After a small in-person funeral at the graveside (thanks to COVID rules) with 10 of her family, followed by a much larger memorial service on Zoom with friends from around the world, Mom and I started looking through some of Nan's belongings – of which there were *many*. While examining bags of paperwork, random receipts and notebooks, we discovered a slip of paper, almost hidden in between the pages. 'SCOTLAND', in all caps, handwritten sideways in red pen marked the edge. Next to it, in list form, were the names of Scottish places and the odd additional piece of information. It was Nan's handwriting, but certainly not from recent years; the writing had a confidence and energy to it. The list read as follows:

Cromarty Firth

X – ALCAIG

Fort William

ULLAPOOL

X – DINGWALL

TAIN (tea on way north)

Latheron

Gunn Museum

John O'Groats

Orkneys

Nairn, lovely seaside town along coast from Inverness

Then to Fort George & back to Alcaig

Home via Glenrothes

Thru Cairngorms & Grampians

Mom recalled that it must have been a list of places Nan had planned to visit when she and her sister took a trip together in their late seventies. This was the first I'd heard about it – I was just seven when the journey took place, but Mom explained that Nan – by this time a widow of almost two decades – had been talking to her sister, Hazel – also a widow by this time – about how she'd always fancied visiting Scotland and seeing the Gunn museum, a heritage centre that tells the story of the Clan Gunn, to investigate her Scottish heritage. Determined Aunty Hazel apparently took no time at all to volunteer to drive and start planning the trip.

Nan's relationship with her sister was like something you'd read in a cheesy novel. Older by five years, Nan was ecstatic when her little sister arrived, and they were inseparable growing up. One of my favourite photos of Nan as a young woman is of the two of them, smartly dressed in 1940s-style dresses, arm in arm and laughing. I remember visiting Aunty Hazel often when I was younger, with Mom and Nan, and the two of them would catch up and natter for hours.

I never met my Granddad, David, who died in 1985, aged just 59. Yet, I feel like I know him. Nan would reminisce about their life together and what a wonderful person he was. Mom would talk to me of the type of father he was – a kind, funny and loving one. Others who knew him as a friend have only good things to say about him. Nan had many pictures of him on shelves and walls at home, and his face became so familiar that it was as though a part of him lived in the house with us. Mom inherited his thick, curly hair. Fortunately for me, the gene was passed on to me, too.

When Aunty Hazel's husband, Brian, died, she and Nan found that they now had another thing to bring them closer together. So, when Nan asked her dear sister about travelling North, the answer was obvious.

According to Mom, some in the family were a little concerned about the concept of two women in their late seventies travelling to Scotland alone, but nothing would deter them. They soon set off in 2002, took lots of photographs, sent home postcards and by all accounts had a lovely time.

Fast forward 20 years and seeing this list of Scottish places triggers an idea in James' brain.

'What if we took a trip like this one?'

I look up from the list to see James's face, his mind clearly full of ideas. Based on previous discussions about the types of holidays we could take this year, I ask, hesitantly, 'Do you mean camping?'

I've never 'properly' camped, which, in my mind, consists of a thin tent blowing in the wind in the middle of a field, so the thought of my first experience being a long trip, wild camping in a likely-to-be-very-cold Scotland full of midges isn't that appealing.

James senses my apprehension. 'Well, we could hire a campervan or something like that.' That sounds better.

'What if we tried to follow the route that Nan took? We could mark down the places she and Aunty Hazel visited and copy it, and I could try and learn more about their trip?'

'Actually, what if we went in Vera?'

As soon as James utters this thought, it's like the twinkly idea lights in my brain all switch on at once. Vera could become the perfect campervan.

Pinterest is searched, videos are watched and articles are read in the weeks that follow this discovery. We find a great company that provides an all-in-one campervan conversion kit for vans like Vera. One wooden trunk that folds out into seats, a bed and a table, with cooking equipment and storage too. All you have to do is fold forward the front seats, fold down the back seats and pop the box in the boot. Simple. Just one hitch – the price. For a kit to suit Vera, we're easily looking at spending £3,000. We don't have that kind of money in our back pocket. All too soon, it seems that this is the end of the dream. I guess we'll have to camp after all.

Thankfully, before a tent is bought and rucksacks are purchased, James decides that he might have a solution. One weekend afternoon, after more longing looks at photos of the box kit and helpful diagrams and dimensions on the company's website, James glances up from his phone and looks at me.

'I could make that.'

2

TRANSFORMING VERA

In the first year of the pandemic, with its lockdowns and don't-visit-anyone rules, we have a little more time on our hands than we normally would. As a result, James gets to work designing our very own campervan kit for our very own Vera. We measure dimensions, find as many photos of existing solutions as we can for reference and start buying materials.

As we're a little strapped for space in our one-bed flat, in September 2020 we take the opportunity to housesit for James's Mom and Dad, Vince and Judith, while they're away for a few days and make use of their garage and tools. While I enjoy the luxury of a carpeted floor, a dishwasher and a beautiful garden, features lacking in our Birmingham home, James starts work putting together the main structure of the campervan. He measures, cuts and joins large rectangles of ply over the weekend. By the time we're due to return home, a base with two benches on either side has been produced, as well as a drawer that slides out from under one of the bench seats. I hop onto one of the bench seats in the back of the van, grinning at our progress, and James takes pictures of me to send to the family.

It turns out that using 18mm ply to build a 1,150mm x 730mm box and three bed slat panels makes for a very, very heavy structure. We need to lose some weight if we want to keep Vera happy and make it easier for us to move the pieces and take them out again as needed. Borrowing a hole saw and circular saw, James removes large lengths from the pieces of wood that will make up the bed base. I'm granted the dusty job of sanding the edges. Thanks to COVID, I have plenty of masks available, and after decorating the floor with wood dust, we now have slightly lighter, and smoother, bed slats.

Once we've added hinges, a drawer and a table leg, we start to feel excited. Even putting the structure on the kitchen floor with the table in position and sitting on the narrow bench seats sandwiching the table top, it feels like our plans might actually come to fruition. A coat of leftover blue-grey emulsion from decorating our flat makes it look slightly less rustic, and the added touch of a piece of surplus vinyl flooring (thanks to my adopted second parents Lee and Vicky) adds a nice finish to the space underneath the table and seats.

The greatest hurdles at this point are 1) finding places to store the large sections in the limited space available at our flat and 2) moving them from the flat to Vera. We decide to keep the main structure under the bed, which provides even more hiding places for Gordon, our cat, who immediately investigates and curls up in the cavity under one of the bench seats. The bed slat pieces slide behind our chest of drawers, pushing the unit a little further into the room and creating a fine opportunity to bump into it when entering, but it's the only place they'll fit.

With the structure complete, we now need cushions to make it comfortable. We require enough to form a large rectangle that we can sleep on, but it needs to be in enough pieces to form seat cushions and back cushions when sitting at the table. Maths is more a strength of James's than mine, so he takes the helm and establishes what shapes and dimensions we'll need. Rather than buy sections of foam, which would have been expensive, James finds a foam mattress in Ikea that perfectly fits the dimensions of the campervan kit when laid out as a bed. All we need to do is to cut it up into the sections required. Sounds simple enough, surely?

After the mattress arrives and we roll it out on the floor – there are few things as satisfying as watching a mattress expand after being tightly curled up – we unzip and remove the white fire-retardant cover and draw lines on the foam to show where to cut. Armed with nothing but a large kitchen knife, and not taking the appropriate amount of time to really think about the process, we start slicing away. Now, foam has an annoying habit of expanding as you cut it, so the end product isn't exactly 'refined', but it does the job. We have six sections of foam of differing sizes that come together to create a full-size double bed. I look down at the discarded cover on the floor.

'Do you think we could use the cover for something?'

James looks puzzled. 'Like what?'

'What if I cut it up and use it as blinds for the windows?'

James has barely nodded his head in agreement before I'm running out of the flat, down the iron stairs that lead from our home to the car park and cutting out window templates using scraps of cardboard. I have to admit in my rush of excitement that they aren't the most accurately sized window covers, but, again, they do the job. They certainly won't be blackout blinds, though. The white material and thin wadding will do little more than prevent passers-by from peeking in, but I figure that that's all we really need… we both sleep fairly well without needing the room to be completely dark, so hopefully we'll be just fine.

After a trip to Aunty Davina's and receiving an excellent lesson in cushion covering, using some beautiful surplus black suede material from Aunty Rachel (we won't say no to free material), we're almost good to go. It has taken almost two years in total to finish.

3

PRACTICE MAKES PERFECT – ALMOST

To test our creation, we plan a weekend away at a nearby campsite with Vince and Judith. In April 2022, we stay at the Cuckoo Farm campsite near Rutland, which doubles as a working farm with a lambing shed. Vince and Judith have also created benches and a bed in their work van, using the remains of old cupboards and trunks from their summerhouse. When they pull into the campsite and pitch up, I can't help but admire the ingenuity of how they've created a makeshift campervan in their Citroen Berlingo, almost identical to our van with the exception of a lack of windows in the back. This means that once they close the doors and tuck in for the night, they're essentially in a black box.

I'm not claustrophobic or afraid of the dark, but reflecting on this makes me grateful to have windows that open on the sides of our van and rear doors with windows that allow us to see the view while lying in bed. We set up the campervan so that the table is up and we can rest our cups of tea on it. Although it's April, it's unusually cold. James pulls out the drawer containing our gas stove and takes out a saucepan to heat up water for tea.

While waiting for the warmth of a mug of tea in my hand, sitting in our van enjoying the peaceful sounds of the countryside, an issue arises that we hadn't foreseen in our designs of the campervan drawer. Sometimes it's not until you use something for the first time that you realise a glaring mistake that was there the whole time. As James sets up the stovetop, and thankfully before igniting the gas burners, it becomes apparent that the wooden sides around the stove, designed to keep the cooker in place, are too high. Even on a low heat, there's a risk that the flames from one of the rings might catch them. As much as I want to test out every element of the campervan, I also don't fancy burning down the very thing we've spent two years on and haven't yet been on the trip we wanted to do in it.

Ok. We'll have to sort that one out when we get home. In the meantime, Judith has set up their camping stove and kettle, which work beautifully, and we're soon sat together with tea in hand and happy, smiling faces. Wrapped up in our big coats, we chat about the vans, get some dinner on and watch the clear baby-blue sky turn into dark indigo, fading into peach as it dives toward the horizon.

We retire to our own vans, transforming the camper into a bed and crawling under the duvet. We've brought our 'winter' 10.5-tog duvet thinking it will be more than enough to keep us warm on a chilly night in the van. Wrong. Very wrong. I'm usually a warm sleeper; I like to have the windows open all year round, and I still feel toasty. But this night is painfully cold. Drifting in and out of sleep, barely feeling my toes, and my nose feeling like an ice cube, I try to cuddle up next to James, but as I move from my position, I have to cross the frozen space between us, making me feel even colder. We brought a blanket and sleeping bag as backups, and James had the good sense to at least put the blanket over us, but he's turned around so much in his sleep that it's no longer covering me at all. In the blackness of night, frozen, I hear the baas and bleats of sheep nearby.

By the morning, I'm beginning to thaw as the sun comes through the window and warms the van. When James wakes, he listens as I reveal the shocking night I've had and gracefully apologises upon learning that he's a blanket stealer. We then agree to add a layer of sleeping bag the next night. As I walk up to the shower block, I look at the happy sheep in the pen next to it and spy two new arrivals. The new lambs are wobbly on their feet and stick close to the others. Very cute.

We have a lovely day with Vince and Judith exploring the cafes and antiques shops of Oakham and return in the evening to make dinner and enjoy the warmth of a firepit between the two vans. Stinking of smoke, we each take to our bed-converted vans and settle down for the night. Thanks to a cosy layer of sleeping bag between us and the duvet, James and I enjoy a warmer night and wake up to a view of trees and fields and the sound of even more new lambs. We could get used to this.

Three months later, we're still not entirely sure when we'll book our Scotland road trip, but we're up for another test run, and thankfully we have friends who are willing to come with us. Caleb and Izzy have also made adjustments to their van so that they can camp in it. However, theirs is a spacious new VW Transporter, in which they've created a bed in the back. The design means they can't quite close the doors when the bed is fully laid out, but it's set to be a warm weekend, and with a gazebo covering the rear, they'll still have privacy. We have to admit we're a little jealous.

This trip proves to be extremely helpful. Unlike the cold, damp weekend with Vince and Judith, this weekend is *hot*. Pushing 35°C, we're forced into shorts and t-shirts. Despite being on the same campsite as before, the difference in weather makes for a contrasting experience. During the day, we sit by our vans under the shade of our newly bought shelter, drinking cold beverages and listening to the sound of happy families on the site. Bliss. Thankfully, the evenings cool down and we're able to sleep comfortably under our 4.5-tog summer duvet. At the end of a weekend of gentle strolls, games and food, we pack up and head back home, waving to our friends as we trundle back up the dusty, rocky track and away from the site.

Just a month later, we're off again in Vera for one final weekend away. We're now starting to get an idea of when we'd like to do our Scotland trip – late Spring 2023. For now, we've booked a couple of days in Louth to spend with James' Aunt and Uncle, Barbara and Steve, who'll stay in their brand-new caravan. Actually, 'brand new' doesn't quite cut it. We arrive to the site first, receive a guided tour by the extremely friendly couple who run it and pull into our assigned bay. The site has gravel pitches, with mown grass in between and a circular path that leads you around the site and back to the exit. Our pitch is immediately on the left, next to an empty one that will house Steve and Barbara when they arrive. Within half an hour, a sparkling, just-been-washed caravan rolls up, towed behind Uncle Steve and Aunty Barbara's Land Rover Freelander.

We learn that they only picked up the van on the way to us and have yet to put any items in it. Thus, the rest of the evening is spent arranging furniture, making the bed and putting pots, pans, plates and cutlery away. James and I prepare dinner, and we're soon happily eating at a camping table under our gazebo.

It's our fifth wedding anniversary in a few days, and our camping buddies for this weekend make us feel very loved. We're surprised with a beautiful card and a large, wrapped present. Carefully, we unwrap the mysterious object to discover a set of side panels for our gazebo. We're over the moon – this is something we've been after for a while. Excited by our new gear, James and I start to attach the sides while Steve and Barbara head back to their caravan to wash up.

When I'm halfway through attaching my side of the gazebo, I glance toward James, who's attaching another side, and I can see we're thinking the same thought.

'These aren't the sides for this gazebo, are they?' I whisper.

James grimaces and shakes his head.

We decide to tell Steve and Barbara, who are understandably devastated that their surprise present isn't quite right. Thankfully, they'll be able to return it. James finds the sides that fit our gazebo online, and soon they're on order, ready to be used at our anniversary party in a few weeks' time.

After a lovely couple of days exploring the seaside and enjoying a pool table located at the campsite, we fold the campervan down – we're getting quicker at doing so now – and feel satisfied that we're Scotland-ready.

4

THE WHEN AND THE WHERE

It's already November, two years and seven months since Nan passed away, and we need to start making real plans if we're going to take this trip in late April or early May of next year, 2023. So, one Sunday morning, we dust off the large map of Scotland we'd ordered online many moons ago and lay it out on the dining table. James finds the photo of Nan's list of place names, and I grab my box of Sharpies. On the map, we use a blue pen to circle the places that Nan had written down, which reveals that her trip was much more based around the east of Scotland than we thought. Places we want to add to the journey are circled in red, and a route begins to form.

Thanks to a beautiful book about camping in Scotland that was gifted to us two years ago, for our third wedding anniversary, we start to get an idea of where we could camp along the way. The book is called *Take the Slow Road: Scotland*, by Martin Dorey, and it was a very welcome present from Luke and Dani, James' brother and sister-in-law. Martin Dorey knows his stuff. It's a gorgeous guidebook, full of routes you can take to tour Scotland and brilliant illustrations, which inspires me to do the same when we go on our own trip. It handily lists good places to camp along the way, which I start to mark on the map.

We can't be certain, but it looks like Nan and Hazel mostly travelled along the east of Scotland and came back down the same way. Many of the places we'd like to see while we're up there can be found on the west coast, so we decide to do a circular route, heading to Glasgow and then following the coastline, hopping onto Skye for a day or two before returning to the mainland and driving the coastal road all the way to John O'Groats.

When plotting the key areas on the map, we realise that much of this journey takes in the North Coast 500 trail – something that has both positive and negative points, it turns out. One positive is the fact that most of the locations offer decent campsites due to the number of visitors that travel the route throughout the year. A negative is that it might well be a busier and more expensive route. We hope that it's a little quieter when we go, but we'll have to wait and see. We don't want to go any earlier, as it's likely to be on the colder side, yet the later we leave it, the more chance there is that we'll get eaten alive by the midges, although I'm yet to meet two people who can agree on what time of year is the worst for midges in Scotland.

Part of Nan's trip included visiting the Orkneys, so as we reach that point on the map, I ask James if we can go there too. Very quickly I get my answer. It's £170 just to get onto the island. That's without adding the costs we'd face regarding food, camping and the likely event of finding ourselves in a gift shop. We abandon the thought of trying to get to the Orkneys this time, instead deciding to use our funds to make the most of experiences on the current route and perhaps a nice hotel stay on our last night. It's a shame, as I'd wanted to visit as many of 'Nan's places' as possible, but to complete the trip, we need to consider our finances. The Orkneys will have to be shelved for another holiday.

Weeks later, sitting at our dining table, with a now slightly torn and crumpled map of Scotland taking up almost all of the surface area, it's a little overwhelming to realise just how many campsites we need to book. To travel the distance we want to in just two weeks, we've planned to go to a different site every night. Fourteen nights. Fourteen sites. I open a new page of my bullet journal. Down the left-hand side of the page, I list the days and dates for the two weeks we'll be away. Our trip will start on the first of May 2023. And it's a Monday. It always pleases me when the first of the month falls on a Monday.

Our first Scottish campsite will be Ardfern Motorhome Park, a beautiful site on the edge of a sea loch that's recommended in *Take the Slow Road*. From the moment I saw the site's website and watched the short video showing the spectacular view, I knew that's where I wanted to go. Thankfully, James agrees, so we book it.

Google Maps tells us that it will take between seven and eight hours if we were to drive straight there from our home in Birmingham. As much as I love to travel – give me a long train journey any day – this trip is a special one, and I don't want to start off with a lengthy trip that won't leave us much time to enjoy the scenery once we get there. So, we decide to stop about halfway in the Lakes, somewhere close to both our hearts.

James has fond memories of family trips to the Lake District, and we honeymooned in the beautiful Coniston. James starts digging and finds a lovely little campsite near the top of the Lakes, overlooking Blencathra, that's relatively cheap compared to what we've seen for most of the sites in Scotland. We pay a £5 deposit, and I record it in my journal.

Most of the other sites are straightforward. Some are sourced from the *Slow Road* book and others through Google or camping apps. The trickiest location to decide on is Skye. It's a shame we'll only be stopping there for one night; there's so much to do and see. There are several options we can choose from when it comes to camping on Skye. Of course, we could attempt to wild camp, but as it will be our first road trip in the van, we agree to opt for sites that give us the opportunity to shower and cook. I find a stunning-looking site near Dunvegan, toward the top of the island and overlooking Little Minch, a strait that forms part of the Inner Seas off the west coast of Scotland. We select an electric hook-up option, which will allow us to use our two-ring electric hob. The hob, as well as a roof box, was kindly gifted to us by a generous couple whom we love.

After a few days of planning and booking, we've chosen eleven sites, and we're now looking at Edinburgh. To complete our Scottish journey, we think it'd be nice to splash out on a hotel for the two final nights in Scotland. Very quickly, however, this looks to be out of the question. Either something's going on in the city at the time we're planning to go or Edinburgh is much more expensive to stay in than we thought, as we're looking at around £200 per night, minimum. Somewhat disappointing, as we've done well so far with our bookings; my bullet journal page is full of dates, locations, site names and prices. And we're tired too. Better not to rush a decision, so we box up the plans for the finale of the trip to be reopened on another day.

On a Tuesday afternoon, I'm working at my desk in the corner of our flat, finishing a proofreading job. James has just got in from a day's window cleaning and is chiselling away at a section of the campervan on the kitchen table. He's trying to create slots for the electric hob's cables.

In three weeks, we'll be leaving for our first night in the Lake District before making our way to our first Scottish campsite at Ardfern. There are still a few things that we want to sort out before we go. The most pressing include booking a night or two at a hotel in Edinburgh and a final site in the Lakes on the way home, arranging for Vera to have a full service to ensure she can take us to the top of Scotland and back again, painting the bed slats of the campervan and buying camping cutlery and a wetsuit.

I've got a half-length wetsuit, which I bought on a family trip to Devon last year. I opted for a shorter one at the time because I was worried about getting too warm while wearing it. My anxiety has the fun habit of being triggered by overheating, and being encased from my neck to my ankles seemed a bit risky. I didn't fancy panicking in open waters. However, once in the water, I realised that there was little chance of getting overheated. The seas off the British coast aren't often warm enough to want to dip your toe in, let alone wear anything less than a full wetsuit. I love being in the water, so I want to make the most of our Scottish adventure and swim when I get the chance. The waters will be even colder than I've probably experienced before, so a full wetsuit should allow me to enjoy the wild water without turning blue. While James chisels and saws away, I hop onto the computer and search for wetsuits. First, I search for kids' sizes. Being five feet and one inch tall has its perks occasionally, and it turns out that many clothing stores class my size as that of a large child. Still, after searching for a while, I find myself turning towards the cost-effective option of a Sports Direct wetsuit, which my sister-in-law and James's sister-in-law both own. I'll join the club.

In the days and weeks that follow, we complete small purchases and minor jobs on the van. James adds a self-adhesive carpet material to the inner metal framework, making it feel cosier. We also buy a Trangia camping stove – recommended by friends of ours who are well-seasoned campers. It's advertised as a 'durable and stormproof' stove, which neatly packs away. It'll be handy to have electric and non-electric cooking options.

About a week before we're due to leave for the first stop in the Lake District, we begin the mammoth task of packing – two weeks' worth of clothes for all weathers, cooking items, safety equipment, hygiene products, bedding and dry food. As it piles up in our hallway, I start to wonder how it will all fit into our small van. Unfortunately, we're unable to transfer everything into Vera until the day we set off, as we're out all day on the Sunday before we're due to leave. To avoid manically and stressfully rushing to pack the car on the Monday of our trip, we agree to get up reasonably early, calmly pack the van and then set off on our adventure feeling nothing but excitement.

On the Sunday evening of the last day of April, I'm almost too excited to sleep. After years of planning, tomorrow is the big day. I wish I could call Nan and let her know.

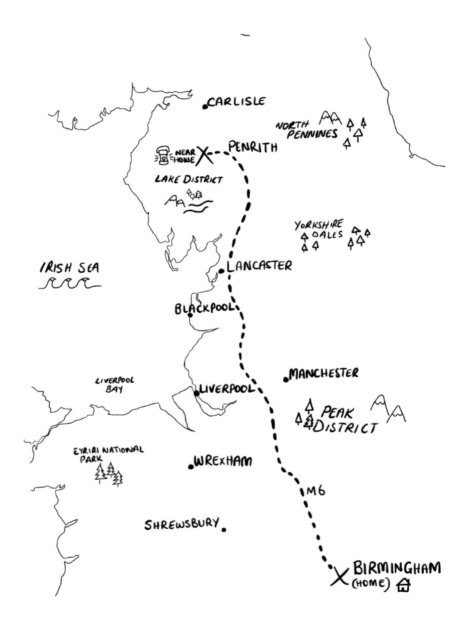

CARLISLE

NORTH PENNINES

NEAR HOME ✗ PENRITH

LAKE DISTRICT

YORKSHIRE DALES

IRISH SEA

LANCASTER

BLACKPOOL

MANCHESTER

LIVERPOOL BAY

LIVERPOOL

PEAK DISTRICT

EYRIRI NATIONAL PARK

WREXHAM

M6

SHREWSBURY

BIRMINGHAM (HOME) ✗

5

DAY 1 – AND AWAY…

After an awful night's sleep thanks to a post-midnight firework show and an engine-revving, car horn-blowing party in the street outside the flat, the idea of heading north feels wonderful. There are a few things to pack in the car before we leave, and we take it leisurely. We want to start this mini adventure feeling calm and happy. Our aim is to leave by 11 am. This will hopefully give us time to load up the car and miss any rush hour traffic. We carry bedding, clothes, shoes, food, coats, art supplies, backpacks and campervan cushions down the iron steps from the flat to the car. The numerous trips up and down the stairs certainly help to wake me up.

We triple-check that we've brought everything, quizzing each other. Finally, we strap ourselves into the front seats. I take a couple of excited selfies to send to Mom to let her know we're on our way.

James edges the car out of the car park to the rear of our flat, and we drive toward the M6, exchanging glances every few minutes as if to say,

'Are we really, finally doing this?' This first leg should take us about three hours and 15 minutes. The van feels heavy, weighed down with a full roof box, the campervan kit and plenty of clothes and food. We don't push Vera. Cruising in the slow lane at about 60 mph is fine with us. We stop twice – once for lunch and once to use the loo. At about 3 pm, we begin to catch sight of the Lake District, the sun highlighting the green, brown, red, yellow and orange hues of the hillsides. Fields of sheep come and go on each side of the motorway. Eventually, we turn off the main road and onto a steep, stony path up to the Near Howe campsite in Penrith. I'm driving, and although I enjoy being behind the wheel, I'm glad to have James's encouragement and guidance as I tackle the lumpy, bumpy, twisty incline until it flattens out.

The site is empty. So much so that I initially drive past the entrance to the field, not realising that the vacant hilltop area to our left is our home for the night. I check my emails and confirm that we've been allotted Pitch 1. James opens the gate, and I drive onto the short green grass, trying not to be distracted by the glorious views I'm presented with while attempting to park strategically. Once I pull up, I practically jump out of the van. Looking out from the rear of the van, the slopes of Blencathra, one of the most formidable climbs in the Lakes, feature on the right. To the left is a gorgeous valley – Troutbeck – nestled between the sun-kissed slopes of other peaks. The wind has picked up, so it's a little chilly while we explore the site. I fold my arms against myself to retain some warmth as we wander toward the brick building that contains the site's facilities.

There's just one toilet and shower for all camping guests, and although there are only five or six pitches here, I can picture myself, legs crossed, waiting to use the facilities while someone else is in the shower. I tell myself not to worry; we might end up being the only campers tonight. At least the room is nice and tidy. The toilet is spotless, and the shower looks as though it's only just been cleaned. Before 2020, I'd have appreciated such a clean bathroom, but I wouldn't have taken too much notice if something wasn't gleaming. After more than two years of a global pandemic, I find that I'm much more aware of fingerprints, marks… anything that suggests potential contamination with a virus.

Trudging back, still hugging myself to keep warm, we see that the van is on a slight slope, so we'll need to get the wheel chocks to level it out. James opens the side door and steps onto the door, reaching up to unlock the roof box. After wrestling with the lock and key, he throws the two chocks onto the ground. I help to position them behind the front wheels while he jumps into the driver's seat and prepares to reverse. I step back a few feet and eye up the situation. James releases the handbrake and slowly reverses. I watch as he brakes, with the wheels mid-way up the chocks. When he engages the handbrake, the wheels glide down to the ground again. Time for a second attempt. This time, I tell James to stop when the wheels are right at the top of the ramps, almost to the point of going over. Cautiously turning off the car again, Vera thankfully only drops by a couple of steps and is completely level. We'll be able to sleep perfectly horizontally tonight.

Opening the back doors, we start to set up the campervan for the first time. I roll the front seats forward, rotating the seat adjusters on the inside of both until the headrests sit on the dashboard. We move the bedding, which had been neatly folded on top of the bed slats in the back, onto the front seats so that we can fold out the slats to form benches. Soon, the drawer is pulled out, the Trangia is set alight and two mugs are sat waiting to be filled with hot, steaming tea.

We sit in the van with tea in hand, soaking in the view. It's hard to believe we've only got this evening to enjoy this site. I realise now how busy the next two weeks will be, hopping from one campsite to the next every single day. I hope it won't be too much. I really want to enjoy this trip and make some happy memories while remembering Nan. As we silently sit next to each other in the van, James slightly stooped to fit under the roof, we gradually hear more and more birds chirping all around us. The sheep in the adjacent field bleat away. Bliss.

I find my art supplies from among the bags and boxes and make a small sketch of the view from inside the van, adding watercolour over the top. The sketchbook I packed isn't really designed for painting, so the paper wrinkles a little as I wet it with my paintbrush. Still, it comes out ok, and I feel happy to have created an artistic memento of our first afternoon of the holiday.

Until this point, James and I had been enjoying having the site and the view all to ourselves, but just before starting dinner, we hear the sound of wheels crunching up the rocky slope we ascended a few hours ago. A VW Transporter winds its way up the track and through the wooden gate to our left. Inside it are a couple, perhaps in their early fifties, and the most adorable black cocker spaniel. When the van stops and the couple exit the vehicle, the curly-haired dog hops out of the van and excitedly runs around, exploring its new surroundings. I smile as I watch its ears flapping about with every turn, jump and sprint.

James has been looking forward to using the Trangia to cook dinner, so he asks if I mind if he cooks for us tonight. Obviously, that's fine with me. I'm beginning to feel my usual first-night-in-a-new-place anxiety, so I'm happy to sit back with our weighted blanket and breathe in the clean air. James sets the Trangia fuel alight and places a saucepan on top.

In no time, we have bowls of hot pasta on the table. Sat on opposite sides, knees touching, we tuck in. While James has to slouch somewhat, my deficiency in height allows me to sit comfortably upright. I look over James's shoulder and spot a third van arriving – a large, grey Citroen Relay – which pulls up behind the cocker spaniel's van.

When the light begins to dim, we walk to the sink area to wash up. Passing the grey Citroen, we wave to the young blonde couple who sit by its open side door and their two golden retrievers.

'They're beautiful,' I say, motioning toward the dogs.

'They're siblings – although you wouldn't know it,' explains the fair-haired woman, legs crossed in her folding chair. 'They're from different litters, and this one,' she says, pointing to the one sitting happily at her feet, 'is the big sister.'

The younger retriever bounds around the van as we continue our walk to the facilities block.

Thankfully, there's plenty of hot water at the sink for washing up. We stand together, James washing and me drying. Behind us are wall-mounted shelves containing numerous DVDs and books – all the usual titles you often see at campsites or holiday lets. There are even a couple of games. But I doubt we'll have time for Connect Four this evening.

The repetitive motion of taking an item from James, drying it and placing it down allows me to ponder where we are and what we're doing here. I try not to drop the plate James hands me while I run through our itinerary in my mind. Tomorrow, Ardfern. Then, Skye. After that, follow the north coast.

The wind has dropped by the time we get back to the van, making for a beautiful evening. I grab my journal, James peruses *Take the Slow Road*, and here we are. I can't believe how much I write. I just don't want to miss anything out; I know I'll forget things as soon as I go to sleep. While I'm writing, we hear the couple next to us trying to capture their dog to put her in the van for the night. The dog's name is Bessie. And it appears that she's mildly disobedient, as we look out of our window and see her escape from the van and run toward the third van. I think we'll be hearing 'Come back, Bessie!' a few times tonight. Could be worse.

The sun is clinging to the horizon, slowly disappearing behind the silhouetted Blencathra as I write my last sentences. James is looking out of the rear windows. Without turning his gaze, he says, 'It's not often you get to watch the sun set over a mountain.'

No, it's not.

OBAN

LOCH LOMOND
& THE TROSSACKS

X ARDFERN

BEN
LOMOND

A83

M8

GLASGOW

EDINBURGH

KINTYRE

ISLE
OF
ARRAN

AYR

MERRICK

M74

DUMFRIES

STRANRAER

CARLISLE

NEAR
HOWE

X PENRITH

LAKE
DISTRICT

6

DAY 2 – HELLO, SCOTLAND

I'm surprised to wake up feeling fairly refreshed. Usually, I have anxiety when staying anywhere new for the first time, but I must have been tired from the journey up. It was a little chilly in the night, but not cold enough to necessitate getting the full sleeping bag out. I wake early thanks to the bright morning light and birdsong. We're in no rush today, so James brews up a cuppa and we sit and enjoy it in bed while absorbing the view. Eventually, I make my way to the shower, taking with me my towel, flip-flops, change of clothes and wash bag. Despite my worries, there's no queue to use the bathroom. As I'm enjoying the lovely hot water, I realise I have no shower gel or soap. Did I leave them at home? I look at my bursting wash bag and then remember – I'd put them in James's, as I couldn't fit them in mine. Oh dear. I scrub a bit harder.

We eat porridge in the back of the van before packing up and getting on our way. Google Maps suggests that we're looking at a journey of four hours and twenty minutes. At 10 am, we trundle down the little lane and wave goodbye to Near Howe. Sheep totter along the side of the path next to the van, as if they're seeing us off the premises, and we take it slowly so as not to spook them. After a few minutes on the road, we stop to top up on fuel to avoid the astronomic prices we expect to see on the motorway. The little station we choose is part of a small complex that comprises fuel, a shop, a gallery, a café and a cinema. If only we had more time.

With a full tank of fuel, we make our way onto the M8 and head north. I take over the driving after we stop at a service station on the way. I really enjoy it. James chats to his brother-in-law Alex on the phone, and it's nice to hear them put the world to rights. Finally, we sail past Glasgow, and hills and mountains begin to decorate the scenery. As it's nearing lunchtime, we decide to make a stop near Loch Lomond – a famous freshwater lake known for its beauty and wildlife. The difficulty lies in finding somewhere to pull over for free and from where we can walk down to the lochside with enough space to make and eat lunch. After several stops and starts, we pass the tiny town of Luss and find a layby that provides access to Culag Beach.

I pull over, and we gather bread rolls, eggs, oil, ketchup sachets – taken from the services – and the Trangia. The pebbly beach that we climb down to opens out onto a beautiful view of Lake Lomond to the left and right. We steadily walk across the stones to look for a good, level place to set up the Trangia. We find a large rock with a flattish top and use small stones to level the stove. Soon, three eggs are crackling away on the lit Trangia while I attempt to halve the rolls without the help of a knife or other sharp implement. A pair of ducks waddle toward us, appearing to laugh at my attempts.

All in all, it's a triumph. Hot egg rolls on a peaceful beach, listening to gentle rolling waves? Yes, please. As I take a bite out of my roll, the good feelings temporarily melt away when bright yellow yolk drips onto my black jeans. Excellent. I grab an empty ketchup sachet and try to scrape it off, but it leaves a yellowish, sticky film on my left thigh. I'll have to change. There's no privacy on this beach, so we'll make a toilet stop down the road, where I'll be able to put a new pair of trousers on.

After clearing up, but before heading off, we take a minute to breathe in the moment. We're finally in Scotland, looking out on a tranquil loch. After all those months of planning and years of building a campervan kit, this is what it was all for. We don't know it yet, but there will be so many moments over the next few weeks that we'll forget to take the time to take in, and they'll be remembered only through photos.

Slowly, we clamber back up the slope to the layby. Driving 10 minutes down the road to the end of Loch Lomond, we find a car park, toilets and a café at Tarbet. The car park costs 50p for a short stop, so we pay up and I use the toilets to change out of my eggy jeans. Since we've paid for the privilege of parking, we decide to have a look around. We wander down to the small pier, where large boats are waiting to pick up tourists to take them on a tour of the lake. The water is still, reflecting the slopes and trees on either side of the lake and the clouds above.

There's still quite a way to go, and it's already mid-afternoon, so when we're back in the van, we travel west, winding around the top of Loch Long and carrying on to Loch Fyne. The journey is beautiful. As we climb toward an area known as 'Rest and Be Thankful', the views beyond and behind are stunning. Sweeping hillsides and dramatic peaks feature at every angle.

While we're quietly enjoying the scenic route, weaving through valleys and woodland, we see it. A stag. At the side of the road. Sadly, however, not in the manner in which we were hoping to see one on the trip – standing mightily on a hilltop, large antlers silhouetted against a setting sun. This one is lying on its side, motionless. Its large antlers stand tall from the still body. We slowly drive past, amazed at its size but sad at the sight of it.

'I wonder what the car looks like,' James considers, 'after hitting something that solid.'

We don't have to wait long to find the answer. Seconds later, we drive past a white car with a bashed-in bonnet. There's no sign of the driver. No police tape either. It's like the start of a good mystery novel. I wonder if the driver was hurt – they must have been – and where they are now. Did they flee the scene of the crime? Does this class as a crime? Will the deer be left there, or will someone come and collect it? I hate not knowing the end to a story. Films or books with open endings are the bane of my life. I know that there's no way of knowing what happened in this situation, and that will bother me for some time.

Finally, we head down the side of Loch Fyne, past the Green Castle at Inveraray and all the way to Lochgilphead. We turn north again, trundling through a small village until we find ourselves at Ardfern Motorhome Park.

The site has 12 spaces, and only three are available. We opt for a corner space for now, thinking we can always move if we decide another spot looks to be a better option. The corner lot offers good views of the loch in front and the hills across the water. Plus, it's a little closer to the toilet and shower. Stepping out of the van and walking through the site, we meet Carol and Ian, a friendly couple in their sixties who are sat outside their red VW campervan. The four of us discuss our routes around Scotland, and we ask if they have any suggestions of where to go on Skye – our next stop. They recommend Coral Beach, and I try to remember to research it later. They're heading to Ullapool next, and I wonder if we'll bump into them again.

Looking at the other two available spaces on the site, we concur that we're in the best spot, so we head back to the van to make a cuppa. It's a touch chilly, so we shelter inside, with the doors pulled to, and sip our tea. Suddenly, James nearly knocks my tea out of my hand as he frantically grabs the binoculars from the seat next to him and angles his face to view the sky over the water. I quickly lurch forward to see what it is that has captured James's attention so unexpectedly and see a glimpse of a large, dark bird, moments before it disappears behind a thicket of trees.

Now, one of our goals for this Scotland trip is to see an eagle. I certainly wasn't expecting to see anything close to this mighty bird before we reached the highlands, but James triumphantly places the binoculars on the table and announces,

'A white-tailed eagle. A WHITE-TAILED EAGLE.'

I know I saw white tail feathers and a dark body, and I agree that it was a big bird, but I didn't get a good look. With me unable to back him up on his sighting, James takes out his phone and opens the Collins British Bird Guide app that he downloaded before the trip. We analyse the images of a white-tailed eagle, and there's little doubt. We've seen an eagle. On day two.

We finish our tea, excitedly recording our sighting in the app, before strolling into the village. It's only a 10-minute walk up the asphalt road, passing quaint houses. In the local shop, we buy some apricot jam and a drink to add to our supplies. As we leave, we wave to a couple who we recognise from the campsite and find a barely-there path along the marshy shoreline of the lake, which tests the waterproofness of our boots. We see a heron, an oystercatcher and myriads of gulls. It's an overcast evening, but mild.

With the jam nestled into the food bag and the bottle of flavoured fizzy water emptied into two cups, James puts the electric hob on and starts warming up the now-thawed vegetarian Bolognese we brought from home. Watching him stir the saucepan, I wonder whether I should have put more thought into what dinners we should be eating on this journey, perhaps planning some meals that relate to my Nan.

Many of my memories – and my cousins' memories – of her revolve around food – particularly her roast dinners. Speak to any of Nan's eight grandchildren, and they will tell you about her 'Paxo chicken'. I don't know the origins of this recipe, but whenever Nan would cook a roast dinner at home, the meat was always chicken, but with a twist. Rather than having the stuffing as an accompaniment to the chicken, it coated it. It wasn't until relatively recently that I realised that this was unusual for a roast dinner. However, it was the norm for me growing up, and I introduced James to it, as well as his family. It's now our go-to roast dinner option. I like to think Nan would be happy to know that her Paxo chicken legacy lives on. My cousin Penny fondly remembers Nan's roast potatoes too – seasoned with garlic and salt, she claims that they were 'the best potatoes ever'. And when Nan cooked, how could the evening be complete without her famous trifle? It was no surprise that in the talk given at her Zoom memorial, food was heavily mentioned. I'm not sure if we'll get chance to enjoy a Scottish roast dinner or trifle, but I'm sure they wouldn't compare to Nan's, anyway.

After we eat, we collect our bowls, cutlery and saucepans and walk toward the two-door wooden shack that houses the only toilet and sink, which sits in the middle of the site, its green metal roof not quite blending in with the greens of the trees and grass around. Multi-coloured lightbulbs hang on a wire along the front edge of the roof. There are shells lined up on a small ledge that circles the toilet room. Through the other door, a white butler sink rests on a wooden unit in front of a window overlooking the water. A bottle of Ecover washing-up liquid stands on the side. While the sink is free, James offers to wash up while I sketch and write in my journal.

Tomorrow looks to be another long stretch, but it includes Glencoe, which is one of the places I've been most looking forward to seeing. As I make the bed and try to get changed without the neighbours catching a glimpse, I hear barking. Diagonally across from us is a campervan housing a couple and their three yapping chihuahuas. Their little legs mean they can't jump very high, so their owners are keeping them in a pen at the side of their van, edged with a foot-high border. They've been yapping intermittently all day, but now that it's time for bed, the sound is more noticeable. I hope they don't keep us up.

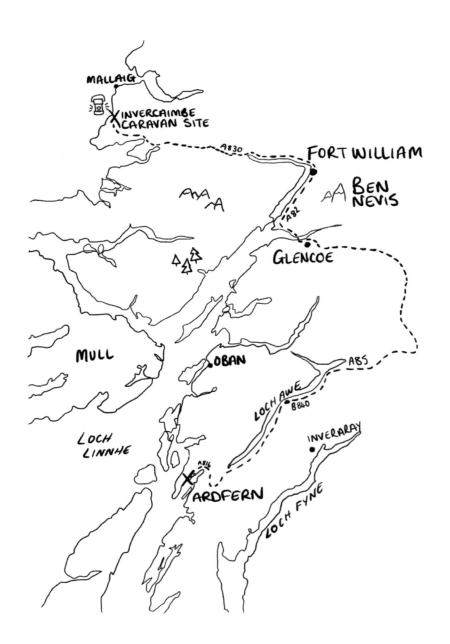

MALLAIG

INVERCAIMBE
CARAVAN SITE

A830

FORT WILLIAM

A82

BEN
NEVIS

GLENCOE

MULL

OBAN

A85

LOCH AWE

B840

INVERARAY

LOCH
LINNHE

A816

ARDFERN

LOCH FYNE

7

DAY 3 – TICKS AND PANIC ATTACKS

As I open my eyes, the grogginess hits me hard. It's early, and I haven't slept well. I felt anxious during the night, and the temperature caught us both out. Despite having the windows open to let in the breeze – albeit a warm one – I woke up several times, desperate to find a cool patch of bedding. People paint a somewhat bleak picture of Scottish weather, suggesting a chilly, damp, midge-filled country, but we're finding the opposite to be true. To look on the bright side, however, when there's only one toilet and shower available, waking up early isn't a bad thing. I drag myself to the foot of the bed and slip my boots on. It's about 7:30 am, and the site is quiet as I walk up to the wooden shed that contains the only shower with my towel, wash bag and change of clothes under my arms. I try to make little noise so as not to disturb the sleeping campers, and I look over my shoulder, beyond the row of vans in front of ours, to the water, which calmly shimmers in the soft light.

The shower is perfectly hot, and I try to dodge making contact with the plastic shower curtain as it gently moves with the breeze that seeps in under the door.

When I return to the van, James is sat on the bed, eating porridge. Since we're both feeling a bit run down this morning, we agree to be a more flexible with our schedule today. We aim to leave at about 8 am to reach Glencoe at a reasonable time. I start packing up while James heads to the shower.

A few minutes later, I look up to see a slightly startled-looking James walking towards me.

'I think I've got a tick bite.'

He lifts his shirt to reveal a tiny tick rigidly attached to his stomach, just below his belly button. I've never seen a tick on someone like this before, and I don't know how to react. I know that there's a specific way you're meant to remove a tick, but I can't remember the details and I don't have any tweezers. Why hadn't I researched this before? I've heard about using a lit match too, but I don't want to risk setting my husband alight either. I find two hair grips and attempt to fashion a pair of tweezers to grip the tick as close to the skin as possible.

It's very stuck, and if it wasn't dead already, it is by the time I give up and James uses his thumb and forefinger to pluck the tiny creature out, leaving a small, almost imperceptible pink mark. As James goes back to the shower to clean the area thoroughly, I sit in the car and Google all there is to know about tick bites. I learn how to determine if a bite will lead to Lyme disease, what symptoms to look for, how long it can take for them to appear. I'm spiralling, reading about the long-term effects of Lyme disease and then applying them to James. I lock my phone and say a prayer to keep me calm. I ask that James be kept safe and healthy. By the time James comes back, I'm calmer. We regroup and agree to carry on as normal but to keep tabs on the pink mark left behind. I take a photo of it for future reference. What novices we are.

As we leave Ardfern, we wave goodbye to Carol and Ian, who are packing up their van. James drives the 68 miles to Glencoe Mountain Resort. On the way, we see highland cows with their fuzzy, golden calves on hillsides. We pass Kilchurn Castle, Ben Lui, Ben Cruachan, Ben Mor and other beautiful peaks, some of which are cloud-covered at their very tops. It's starting to get a touch misty, which only adds to the dramatic atmosphere brought about by the bleak landscape. Finally, we reach Glencoe. It's my first time, and it doesn't disappoint. What an impressive landscape, with towering hills and mountains at every turn. You can also see for miles between them, looking over barren, brown, heather-covered ground. Arriving at the mountain resort, I change into my waterproof trousers, as the rain is coming in.

'It's a wee Scotch misty at the top', explains the ticket officer for the chairlift up the mountain. We hop onto the lift, and I try not to look down, gripping the cold metal safety bar in front of me.

The views are overwhelming. It's a shame the weather has closed in, but it doesn't stop the mighty landscape from making us feel ridiculously small. We take some selfies and photos on the way up, including the stream beneath our dangling feet that trickles down the mountainside. At the top, we wander around the level area, scanning the horizon. Mountain bikers dismount from the lift and make their way back down the slope. They're all really young. And muddy.

There's not a huge amount to do or see at this mid-level of the mountain, and the chairlift doesn't go any further up at this time of year. So, after strolling around in the misty air, we get back onto the lift and slowly trundle down, watching bikers dart around muddy corners. James is quiet, but he smiles at me when I ask if he's ok. Maybe he's just tired.

It's lunchtime when we return to ground level, so we order some lunch at the café, with its steamed-up windows and damp visitors warming up. By the time my soup and James's sandwich arrive, James is starting to feel unwell. We sit at a table in the café, but I can tell James isn't comfortable. He needs air, so I hurriedly try to gather up our plates, cutlery and drinks and follow him out of the door. I drop a knife as I try to manoeuvre my way out of the door. I find James at a table, his face pale and his knee bouncing. Within a few minutes, James has a panic attack.

I've decided not to write too much about it because although it was awful watching James try to push through the panic and uneasiness that comes with an attack, it didn't ruin the highlights of Glencoe. At the end of this day, James will tell me how guilty he felt about how he was while in one of the places I'd been so excited to visit. But he shouldn't feel guilty. This is what marriage is all about – being there for each other through thick and thin. I know what panic attacks feel like, and it hurts to see my husband experience one, especially on this trip. But James has held my hand plenty enough for me to return the favour now.

James manages to eat some of the lunch we ordered, and a little of the tea, before he heads back to the car. I follow shortly afterwards and find him curled up on the passenger seat, clutching a pillow. I'm worried, but James gives me a thumbs up and nods to say he's okay. I drive the rest of the way.

It's another stunning drive, and the hour and a half to Arisaig flies by. At one point, James needs the toilet, quite urgently, and without anywhere to pull over safely, I end up driving up the verge of a main road without a layby, with all four wheels on the grass. When James emerges from the trees, I turn the key, get into gear and go nowhere. The wheels turn on the spot. I can see mud flying through the air on both sides of the car. I'm starting to get nervous about being stuck, and I don't want James to start having a panic attack again. Thankfully, I remember that we've got chocks in the roof box, so James hops out to get them. Wedging them under the front tyres, I manage to gain some purchase on the chocks and gradually steer Vera back onto the tarmac road, leaving behind trenches on the verge and decorating the van with a significant amount of Scottish mud.

The campsite at Arisaig is lovely. The reviews had warned about the host being somewhat frosty, but as we drive past her on the central path through the site, she helpfully guides us to our pitch, which couldn't be better. We've got a great view of the beach, and the other visitors seem to be quiet and friendly. After an emotional day, we set up the van quickly, aiming to have some time to sit with a drink, soak up the view, and have a more relaxed evening. For about an hour, we sit with the rear doors open, looking out over the grey-blue water and toward the Isle of Oronsay.

It's a cool but bright evening. I forget that the darkness falls later and later the further north you go. It's still gloriously light at 7 pm as we stroll onto the small, empty, sunlit beach a few metres from the van. The water looks inviting, gently lapping against the dark rocks and golden sand, but dipping our hands in tells us that it wouldn't be the warmest of swims. I have my wetsuit in the car, but I'm enjoying strolling on the sand with James so much that I don't want to disturb this moment anyway.

The sun sets on the horizon, glistening over the rippling water and creating a romantic glow across the rocks. I FaceTime Mom to show her the view and update her on our journey. She can't believe how far away we are.

James and I sit on some rocks and listen to the gentle waves come and go. When we started courting, we often had what we called 'bottle moments' – times we wished we could capture and come back to, and over the nearly six years of being married, countless events have become such moments. Closing my eyes, holding James's hand and feeling a warm breeze brush against my face, I'd bottle up this moment if I could.

Still hand in hand, we return to the van and get out a board game. I need to wash my hair, but with an earlyish ferry trip in the morning, I doubt I'll have time before we leave. So after losing Project L – a simple but beautiful Tetris-style board game – to James, I gather my towel and wash bag and head to the shower block. They're not the worst facilities we'll see on this trip, but the spiders and daddy long-legs scattered in all corners and crevices make for a speedy shower. The tiles are cracked and darkened by years of use. But the water is hot, and as long as I avoid the shower curtain sticking to me, it feels nice to be warm and clean.

I wrap my wet hair with a towel, change into my pyjamas and stroll back to the van, watching the glow of the sunset slowly dissipate behind it. A delightful end to a topsy-turvy day. I sleep the best I have for days. James, on the other hand, has a more restless night. I hope he's back to his normal self soon.

8

DAY 4 – ROCKY ROADING

We wake early, before our alarms. Perhaps our subconscious minds knew that we had a ferry to catch. The ferry to Skye leaves at 9 am, so we climb out of the van with time for a quick wash and toilet visit before packing up and waving goodbye to our favourite campsite so far. As we leave, winding our way out of the site and onto the rocky main road, I glance out of my window and see large brown figures on a nearby mound.

'Wild horses!' I announce, after focusing my sleepy eyes through my glasses.

James, in the driver's seat, turns to look out of my window and sees their long dark manes and tails, contrasted against their chestnut-brown bodies. They sit calmly on the grass, almost hidden by the bright yellow gorse bushes above them and the imposing mountainous peaks in the distance. A dramatic sky looks over the scene, and I hope the weather holds out for the day.

Driving north, we see signs for Mallaig (pronounced 'Mah-leg' – thank you Simon from Ardfern for the clarification). The ferry port is relatively quiet when we arrive, and our empty stomachs were hoping for a small café or shop to grab a bite for breakfast. No joy here, though. We're early, so James hops out of the car to see if there's anywhere nearby that might provide sustenance but returns a little while later empty-handed. We'll have to wait for food; maybe we'll at least get a cuppa on the ferry.

When the small cargo boat reaches the terminal, any hopes of a hot tea or coffee are quickly dashed. There's barely room for a few vehicles, let alone a drinks station. We're one of the first to board the boat, and we leave the van on the ground level to climb up the steps to the top deck. There are a few seats, but most of the travellers, including an Aidan Turner lookalike who caused me to do a double take, stand and watch the waves crash against the boat's sides. The water is relatively calm, but the brisk sea air forces us to pull up our hoods while we watch the mainland fall behind and Skye approach.

Thirty minutes later, we're driving onto Skye, and we grin at each other. But we're also very hungry now and in need of some tea, so we nip into the nearest shop, making a weak and mildly unpleasant tea from the hot drinks machine inside.

We begin the drive towards our first pit stop, the Talisker distillery, sipping cooling tea en route. After a few minutes, the need for food takes over, and we pull into a layby overlooking the sea and set up the Trangia. Soon, porridge is filling our bellies and the sound of sheep in the field that slopes toward the sea fills our ears. We laugh at how some of the sheep are lying. Are they dead? They're on their sides, their legs stretched out as if rigor mortis has set in. But then a flick of an ear or a twitch in the knee betrays their sleeping state. A new game for the holiday: 'Dead or asleep?'

Renewed by hot, oaty goodness, we travel north. Driving through southern Skye is a strange experience. Browner and flatter than I expected. The clouds have parted, leaving a bright blue sky with the sun highlighting the dry, grassy surroundings.

'It feels a bit like Mars', says James.

'It's like we're driving around Arizona', I respond.

Neither of us have been to Arizona – or Mars, if that was ever in question – but there seems to be no other way to describe the scenery. Miles of beige and brown land stretch into the distance, with grey-brown peaks distributed across the horizon. There's certainly a beauty to the bleakness before us, lit up as it is in the beaming sunlight. I wonder how different the landscape appears in the height of summer, when the copper and umber tones transform into luscious greens.

The further north we drive, the greener the fields become and the more rugged and mountainous the view. We take the A87 past Loch an Cairidh and Loch Airnort. A line of cars forms behind us as we meander through the winding roads, but we don't care. We're doing 45 mph in a 60 mph zone, soaking up the scenery. No rush for us.

The roads on Skye. How do I describe them? I thought the potholes and bumps on Birmingham streets were bad, but it would appear the Highland Council has more pressing matters to attend to than the resurfacing of Skye's roads. We'll be fortunate if Vera makes it off this island in one piece. Nearing Talisker Distillery, a sign warns of

'Substandard roads for 10 miles'. An understatement, it turns out. What follows is a long stretch of pothole-ridden, bumpy, suspension-shattering track.

There are plenty of spaces in the car park, which we gratefully pull into after rattling around for so long. The warm sunshine has caught us out today, so we quickly change into lighter clothes. We haven't booked a tour at the distillery, so we know there's little chance of being shown around, but it'll be fun to have a look anyway. The entryway to the distillery is circular, with a 360-degree panorama seascape painted high on the walls around us. A cool feature. It turns out that all we'll be able to see of this famous whisky distillery is the gift shop. The friendly Scot behind the counter explains that tours are generally booked up weeks in advance. It's a shame for James, who's the whisky fan, but at least we've saved some money. We buy an enamel mug and whisky glass with Talisker branding and a small bottle of Caol Ila whisky. It feels a bit cheeky to buy a different whisky to the one made at the distillery we're at, but it's James's favourite, and they're selling it here, so we go for it.

Satisfied with our purchases, we wander out of the distillery and meander down to the lochside, sitting on a group of rocks and breathing in seaweed-scented air. It feels tranquil. Nan didn't make it to Skye, and even if she had, I doubt visiting the distillery would have been on her list of priorities. But as I watch seabirds swoop and glide above the water, I reckon she would have liked this. Peacefully watching the world go by, probably with a milky cup of tea in hand. She'd have liked the one from the petrol station.

Since it's lunchtime, we drive five minutes down the road to Café Cuil

— an absolute gem. The red-roofed building is baked in sunlight, and happy travellers come and go from the double doors on the side. There's a tiny shop attached to the café, containing locally made books, jewellery, cards, household items and more. I take glance inside, clocking a pair of silver oval-shaped earrings I might come back to after lunch.

Despite it being more than two years since the start of the COVID-19 pandemic, the impacts of the lockdowns and social-distancing rules still permeate many of the places we're visiting. Here, we're encouraged to order our food through a QR code stuck to the table we've chosen outside. I opt for the intriguing vegetarian 'Highland Shakshuka', while James orders a bacon and egg toastie. Waiting for lunch to arrive, we sit in the sunshine, sunglasses on, listening to accents from around the world and watching as cars, campervans and caravans pass on the road. The food is delicious. My bowl of eggs, tomatoes, peppers and vegetarian haggis fills me up. It's a happy moment, and James is brighter than he has been for the last couple of days. I nip back into the shop and treat myself to the silver earrings, putting them in as I jog back to the van.

The rest of the journey to Kinloch Campsite is great. We sweep along hillside roads, eye level with birds of prey and grazing sheep that don't seem to notice our big, rumbling vehicle motoring past. We think we spot an eagle after a few minutes of driving and eagerly pull over. On closer inspection through binoculars, it turns out to be a buzzard, something we see quite often in Birmingham. But still a beautiful creature. We drive on.

As we near the campsite, winding down a narrow path and over a small bridge, we can feel the excitement building — the site overlooks a serene loch and is nestled between rocky, mossy hills. Rolling up to the reception building, we check in and are directed to pitch 42. We couldn't have hoped for a better spot. We're right on the water's edge, so we reverse in so that we'll be looking at the vast loch from the back of the van. Within minutes of setting up, James motions toward a dark shape bobbing up and down just a few metres away in the water. We stop and watch a seal plunge beneath the rippling water, resurfacing again seconds later. Its shadowy eyes look around, and soon we see a second seal approach. The friendly pair duck and dive around each other and around the dark rocks looming out of the water.

One of the reasons we chose this site was because of a BBC programme we'd watched, called Take a Hike. A series of episodes was based on Skye, and an interesting walking route began at a stone monument near some ancient church ruins just up the road from here. It only looks like a short walk to the ruins, and we need to pop into a shop to get some milk anyway. So we lock the van and make our way up the road.

The heat is unexpected. Nearly everyone we spoke to about visiting Scotland had warned us of the cold, the rain and the wind we'd likely face. No one suggested that we'd ever be at risk of overheating. In the still air, and under a cloudless blue sky, we climb the incline through the small row of shops and houses, and I regret my choice of leggings, jumper and mac. Ten minutes into the walk, the mid-day sun is warming the top of my head. My hair is hot to the touch. James chuckles as I try to keep up with him on the hill that leads to the crumbled walls of the old church.

When we finally reach it, I find some shade and lean against a wall to cool down. There isn't much left of this building, which was likely once a centre of the community hundreds of years ago. Crooked, weathered gravestones emerge from the ground, and it's difficult to make out many of the names.

Back on the main road, we enter the local shop and pick up some supplies. It's also where we see a local man in a green and blue kilt. I wonder what clan the kilt refers to.

Nan's family name was Gunn, and she always prided herself on being of Scottish heritage. However, after numerous ancestry projects and meticulous research from Mom and my aunties, we've still not found the Scottish link. The Gunn name came from somewhere, but as yet, it's a mystery. I like the Gunn tartan though. It's mainly blue and green with thin red lines crossing throughout. Not dissimilar to the tartan on the man before me, but there's no way I'm going to ask him in the middle of this corner shop.

Returning to base, we observe a new arrival on the campsite, on the pitch next door to ours. A shiny new Land Rover Defender, with a tent box sat on the roof. As we near the side of our van, we see, through the open canvas door of their roof box, that a young couple are reclining inside, watching something on their laptop. James makes looks at me with big eyes.

'I'm only a tiny bit jealous.'

'But we love our little Vera,' I say, opening the rear door.

As much as the trendy young couple seem to be very at home and enjoying an Instagram-worthy camping experience, our trip wouldn't be the same if we hadn't used Vera. For one thing, James built the campervan kit specifically for this van, which makes it feel so personal to us. And on a similar note, I'm conscious of the fact that Nan had seen it and even been driven around in it when she was more mobile. I give the roof a little tap as I reach into the van.

I pull out the drawer that holds our kitchenware. We make curry on the electric stove and then dive into a wedge of carrot cake we bought from Café Cuil earlier. I flick away a tiny tick that I spot crawling up my ankle. For a few moments I frantically brush my legs with my hands – I read enough about Lyme disease to know that I don't want it. It also reminds me to check on James's bite. There's a faint mark where the tick had latched on, but it's no worse. I start to relax. We FaceTime Vince and Judith, updating them on the journey and showing them the view. The evening light slowly dims, and we quietly watch the seals bobbing about. I sketch a lonely house on the opposite bank. We're both feeling content as we tuck ourselves into bed.

9

DAY 5 – CLIMBING UP AND DRIVING OVER

I wake at 4:30 am to a bright light shining through the gap between the edge of the blind and the window frame. Pulling the blind away from the window, I see the moon just about to go down behind the mountains in the distance. A moonset. I can't remember ever seeing one before, and it's beautiful. I don't have my glasses on, so to me it is a bright, white circle, with hazy edges, glowing against a dark blue sky. James stirs beside me, so I gently nudge him awake and show him the sight. It feels like a special, secret moment between us. I mentally bottle up this memory.

By the time the sun rises, the seals are still bobbing about as we roll up the blinds on the back windows and peer out. Our plan for today is to scale the Old Man of Storr – something Alex and Laura have done and highly recommended we do should the chance arise. We agree that we're not in too much of a rush today – the next campsite isn't too far away, so we can take today a little slower.

The showers at the campsite are the type where you have to press a button for water every few seconds. The water is mostly warm. My coral-colour shower flip-flops squelch as I walk back to the van, where James has begun packing away. We leave the table up in the back and trundle our way off the site. It's a shame we don't have longer on Skye – I think a few more days to explore this beautiful island would have been lovely.

Until now, we've used Google Maps a lot on the trip to guide us from site to site, but it often takes us the quickest route – not the most scenic. So this time we use our paper map to direct us. It's a nice journey. Released from the pressure of watching how many miles are left or what time we're due to arrive at our destination, we simply enjoy the view and drive steadily up the island. Quickly, the unmistakable rocky form of the Old Man of Storr comes into sight. It gets closer and closer until we find ourselves at the car park at the bottom of the path that heads to the landmark.

I make cheese sandwiches in the back of the van for us to eat at the top. It's chilly, but the forecast has suggested it would be warm and sunny by lunchtime, so I'm reluctant to layer up. But James asserts that it will be windy as we climb, making it much cooler than we might expect. I wear my walking boots, thick socks, walking leggings, t-shirt, base layer, zip-up fleece and waterproof coat. We start the incline.

It's a steep initial climb. In Take the Slow Road, Martin Dorey makes a funny comment about encountering tourists on hikes like this in completely inappropriate footwear. We soon pass others with interesting shoe choices. Gesturing to a young man in jeans and a hoodie, James laughs, 'If he can climb this in Chelsea boots, you can do it.'

We continue our ascent, and the sun soon breaks through the cloud cover and immediately, the air feels warmer. With every step, I can feel the temperature rising, and even James rolls up his sleeves. Feeling overheated has always been anxiety-inducing for me, and I try to take deep breaths and keep walking. As we turn a corner, I take my fleece off, fold it up and stuff it into James's backpack. I reach for the water flasks and pass one to James. As I try to hold the flask in one hand while tightening the drawstrings on the bag, it slips out of my grasp and falls to the ground with a thud. Water spurts everywhere, even splashing those passing us. I'm struggling in the heat, and I frantically scramble to pick up the flask and save whatever water is left inside. James holds me by both arms and reassures me that everything is fine. He can see that I'm starting to panic.

'We've got another bottle that's still full of water', he reminds me.

I take some more deep breaths, apologise to some walkers who pass us by and start to climb again. I glance behind to see how far we've come already. There are amazing views of the Isle of Raasay. At the next corner, off comes my coat. The steep hike continues, and I have to sit for a moment in James's shadow to cool down and stay calm. After another section, I'm down to my t-shirt. We stop to eat behind a large rock to the side of the path. We add crisps to our cheese sandwiches and smile as we crunch our way through them. Finally comfortable in my now weather-appropriate attire, we head back to the main trail. The wind has picked up again, which is a relief. We drink flask tea that tastes like all flask tea does and carry on walking. In just 10 more minutes we're at the base of the 55-metre-high pinnacle of basalt rock.

It seems to defy the laws of gravity. Surely it'll fall over at some point?

There are many tourists stopping to photograph the rocky formation, so we keep climbing to an area called Photographer's Point. A strong wind batters us as we clamber up a narrow path toward the viewing platform. A fellow traveller is seated by the path, and I can see that the rest of her family have carried on without her. I ask if she's okay as we pass, to which she smiles, nods and states, simply, 'The wind'. I smile and periodically look back to check on her as we near the platform. Eventually, she rises, makes her way to the top and has pictures taken of her with her husband and child.

We take stereotypical tourist photos of each other in front of the Old Man and the Needle. Holding onto each other, we carefully pick our way back down the trail, passing numerous dogwalkers, including an almost breathless woman who's trailing behind a fuzzy Pomeranian.

'If that,' says James, looking at the tiny dog, 'can do this walk, so can Rosie Clifton'. I roll my eyes.

We practically race down the route we climbed. It turns out that being short in stature gives you a handy lower centre of gravity, and I traverse the boulders, stones and steps surprisingly quickly. I'm trotting down the path when I suddenly lose my footing. For all of a millisecond, I see my life flash before my eyes. I catch my balance just as James rushes to grab hold of my arm. We nervously laugh it off. Let's not rely on my lack of height to get me down in one piece, I think.

We reach the bottom in almost no time, but the steep decline has made our legs feel wobbly. Stumbling into the car, we stretch. Suddenly I feel completely exhausted. But there's one more place we'd like to see before we leave this beautiful island – Kilt Rock and the Mealt Falls. They're only 13 minutes up the road, so after changing out of his boots, James starts the car.

'Almost perfect' has become a term James and I use frequently to describe our adventures. Over the years, we've been to some amazing places in the UK on holiday, for an anniversary or just for a day out. And for one reason or another, there's always something that makes the experience not entirely perfect. For example, once, when we went away for our anniversary, we stayed in an adorable Airbnb – a little hut on a farm in the Cotswolds – equipped with a log burner and views of neighbouring sheep. James had bought me a new pair of dungarees, and it was turning out to be a holiday to remember. We went on nice walks, relaxed with tasty food and were generally extremely content. Then I involuntarily performed my party trick. I'd prided myself on having coped with my anxiety well for a few weeks before our holiday. But as many can attest to, anxiety and panic attacks often come without much warning. I've always felt some nervousness on the first night or two of staying somewhere new. But I thought I'd gotten away with it on that holiday.

Trying to get to sleep on the final night, I felt the usual butterflies fluttering around in my stomach, and the sense of dread rising toward my chest. I reached for my bag of anxiety tablets, fumbling to find the one best used for panic. I could feel my temperature rise, and I started to pray. The minutes that passed felt like hours, until I realised that there was nothing I could do to stop the inevitable. I attempted to calmly swing my legs out of bed, make my way down the creaky wooden staircase and step into the cool bathroom. To avoid ruining anyone's dinner, let's just say it was an unpleasant night. At one point, in the early hours on the 11th of August, James smiled at me from the bathroom doorway while I knelt beside the toilet, and whispered, 'Happy anniversary!'. Almost perfect.

Now, after having an amazing time on Skye so far (ignoring the challenges we experienced while climbing up to the Old Man), we're driving down the now familiar bumpy, hole-ridden roads and looking forward to seeing the natural wonder of Kilt Rock on the northeast of the island. On nearing the entrance to the car park, we encounter a sign that tells us work is being carried out in the car park, and the viewing area is closed off. Great. 'Oh well', we say, 'almost perfect,' as we turn around to head back down the east coast.

The views are, once again, incredible, so the hour-long drive to the bridge between Skye and the mainland is a delight. I watch as Raasay, Scalpay and, in the distance, Applecross pass us by over the water. We sail over Skye Bridge and into Kyle of Lochalsh. We make our way to the A890, travelling up the right-hand side of Loch Carron and back down the left-hand side towards our next stop: the Wee Campsite. I can't remember much about the site as we near it; I booked it nearly six months ago. Before driving up the lane that leads to the site, we nip into the Spar shop just around the corner to stock up on supplies. A blackboard sign out the front states 'Hot pizza to order'. Sounds amazing. The idea of getting a hot, takeaway pizza this evening after a beautiful drive from Skye sounds like the perfect end to the day. There's a number you can call to order ahead, so I pick up some porridge, milk and biscuits while James takes note of the pizza toppings available.

We drive up the sloping path by the row of shops, which leads us to the smallest campsite we've seen so far. 'Wee' indeed. Our pitch is the first one we come across, so I hop out to remove the 'Reserved' sign that the owner has thoughtfully left to guard our spot, and James pulls in so that our back windows face the loch, which is beautifully calm. The only things blocking the view are the tops of the shop roofs on the road below and a tall flag, blowing in the wind. It's blue and white, and as my eyes focus, I see that it's the Scottish flag. But there's white writing layered on top too – as the wind blows the flag straight, I see 'YES' in all caps in the centre of the flag.

Being politically neutral, I presume this flag suggests that the campsite owner supports the idea of Scottish independence, but I don't really know. I don't fancy asking the owner either, especially in my Brummie accent.

As I start unpacking the van, I turn to my right and see the owner, Iain, by his car opposite. I wave hello, and when we're settled, Iain comes over and tells James about the facilities and the area. We pay up and then realise that we haven't taken a photo of the number to call for pizza. I'm feeling exhausted by this point, so James kindly walks back to the Spar, orders pizza and comes back. In the meantime, I make tea on the Trangia and sit in the van. I wonder why my head feels heavy, but then I remember that we hiked the Old Man of Storr only this morning. I try not to get too comfortable, listening to the water slowly getting to boil and feeling perfectly warm under a blanket. We drink tea, and half an hour later, James ambles down the path away from the campsite to collect the pizza. In no time, we're eating hot, cheesy slices out of warm card boxes.

Iain had told James about a nice short walk that he recommends to all visitors. It starts at the rear of the site and follows a path leading up to a viewing point, from which you get a magnificent view of the loch and surrounding hills and peaks. My eyelids are heavy, and I'm sleepy, so James takes his phone and goes to explore. It's that gorgeous time of the evening when the light is golden, so part of me wishes I'd gone with him, but as I take out my journal to write my entry for today, even writing feels like an arduous task. However, the words come easily, and I find myself losing track of time as I describe all we've done today, with climbing Old Man of Storr seeming like something we did days ago, not this morning.

Nearly an hour later, the light is fading, and there's no sign of James. I'm sure he's simply enjoying the stroll and is leisurely walking back, but in the quietness of the valley, on a campsite with only one other van, I can feel a worry building. I tell myself that everything's fine – there's no reason to be concerned. Still, I send him a text to ask if he's ok. When I realise the message hasn't gone through, I stop telling myself that everything's ok and start edging my way to the back doors to put my boots on and go and find him.

I'm about to slide my foot into my boot when I look up and see a happy James bouncing down the site toward me. His phone had died. He shows me pictures of the view at the top of the hill, overlooking the entire loch. The images are incredible, and although I've enjoyed spending time writing and recollecting the events of the day, I'm a little sad to not have shared James's experience. James had FaceTimed Alex and Laura while he was at the top too, catching up with them and showing them the beautiful scenery. They sent their love to me.

Since I'm nearly out of the van anyway, I take the opportunity to visit the shower block. The facilities are basic but clean, and if you can put up with the company of rather large spiders in most of the corners, the plentiful hot water makes for a nice shower.

The wind drops, and the odd midge can be seen fluttering around. We tuck ourselves into bed and watch an episode of The Office US on my phone. Looking through the back windows, we see an almost cloudless sky with a bright circle of light appearing over the hills on the opposite bank. A moonrise. The light is reflected over the water in a rippling line toward us. A good day.

AN
TEALLACH

POOLEWE

SANDS
CARAVAN &
CAMPING

LOCH MAREE

KINLOCHEWE

A832

BEINN
ALLIGIN

LIATHACH

HAVE GONE

WE SHOULD

A890

APPLECROSS

THE WEE CAMPSITE

THE WAY

LOCHCARRON

10

DAY 6 – HOW TO AVOID A CORONATION

Most of the UK is preparing to watch the coronation of a new king today. Yet, we wake after a good sleep to another beautiful, peaceful day in Scotland. The sunlight spreads across the hills opposite, and birdsong surrounds us. I check my phone for messages and any significant news. There's a funny BBC News article titled How to Avoid the Coronation. One suggestion is to escape to the country. I think we've taken that about as far as we can. In this tiny village in Lochcarron, there's not even a hint of coronation excitement.

The sun's out, so I apply plenty of sunscreen – too much it seems – I've turned a shade lighter and have patches of white all over my face. James refills our water bottles and says goodbye to the lovely Iain MacRae. Rather than check the paper map, we decide to use Google Maps. Unfortunately, we forget that this next leg we're about to take was meant to include Applecross and the coastal road. Many friends had told us how unmissable Applecross is, and it was meant to be a key part of this trip.

Instead, Google takes us the most direct route, up the A896.

By the time we realise our mistake, it's too late to turn back. The hours of driving between sites have made us tired and forgetful – likely why we didn't think to double-check the route today. Still, the drive is incredible. We may be missing out on some unbelievable sights at Applecross, but we pass a number of small lochs and wind through some magnificent peaks, the tallest of which being Slioch, at 980 m. It towers above the southeast end of Loch Maree, which we drive the length of on our way north. The water is perfectly still, reflecting the sweeping hillsides. Forests of deep green pines stand out against the brown and beige tones of the slopes. As we turn away from the lake, we seem to enter a forest, with trees surrounding the narrow track. The sun is shining, and – despite the disappointment of missing out on Applecross – we are happy.

We drive into Gairloch: a lovely seaside town with a harbour that looks like it hasn't changed in 70 years or so. I wonder if Nan passed this way on her route to Ullapool. We'll be there tomorrow, and I'm excited to find the locations behind some of the photos of her trip, which I've been keeping safe and studying since we left Birmingham. As we join the coast once again and glide down the blessedly smooth road towards Sands Caravan and Camping site, the view is, again breathtaking. The sea is calm, the sun continues to gleam and sheep line the track as though they're welcoming us to our next destination.

Sands isn't quite what I thought it would be. When we found it online after the recommendation in Slow Road, it looked like a quaint site, albeit one of the bigger ones, but somewhere we could relax and enjoy the within-walking-distance beach. As we pull into the entrance area, it takes me back to staying on a large caravan site in Brean, visiting my Dad. Aged 12 or thereabouts. There are lots of families milling about and children running around – a stark contrast to what we've gotten used to and a shock to the senses. Thus far, each site has been quiet in terms of noise, relatively remote, small and calming. While I've been sad not to have enjoyed longer on the other campsites, I'm glad we're only booked for one night here. Pitches are allotted on a first-come-first-serve basis, so we opt for one that's not too far from the loos but in what appears to be a quieter spot, with a beautiful view of the sea. For the first time, we decide to set up the gazebo. It's been sitting, wrapped up in its bag in the roof box, for six days now, so it's about time we got some use out of it. Plus, with so many neighbours, creating a bit of privacy sounds like a good idea.

As it turns out, it's not just the privacy element that benefits us. Within minutes of attaching two of the side panels, we experience the first proper rain of the trip. The rain pelts us as we hurry to open the doors of the van. We bundle ourselves into the back, with faces dotted with water droplets, and sit with the doors open, sheltered by the gazebo. It's not a long shower, but we stop for a few minutes to watch people running to their caravans through rain-streaked windows.

As it eases, we brew up a cuppa and make lunch: a packet of curried chickpeas and grains and some beautiful fresh bread we bought in Lochcarron. After, we make our way to the laundry room with a full-to-bursting bag of dirty clothes, including my black jeans that still have egg yolk on them. At least with larger sites like this one, the facilities tend to be plentiful. Large washing machines and tumble dryers line the room's walls, the big round doors reflecting our faces as we step in. The basic washing cycle is 40 minutes. I shove the clothes into the drum while James pops £3 into the slot. While we wait, we explore the rest of the facilities and are pleasantly surprised by the loos and showers. The well-stocked shop has everything one could need – tick-removal kits, fruit, cheesy seaside-based gifts, swimming gear, mugs. I've been craving something a little healthier, so I pick up an orange. I add ginger tea and more oats for breakfast and pay up.

Our plan was to have more of a chilled day today, so while James goes to collect our washing, I sit and sketch. I draw the Old Man of Storr, attempting to capture the ruggedness of the rocks. James returns with an armful of almost-dry clothes, thanks to a session in the tumble dryer, and I hang them out on the horizontal poles of the gazebo.

For dinner, I make fajitas. The frying pan is slightly warped and doesn't quite sit flat on the electric hob. After several minutes and a distinct lack of sizzling, I change tack and set up the trusty Trangia. The sweet sound of crackling onions fills the gazebo in no time. We eat dinner while watching the Formula One Miami Free Practice 3 on my phone.

Another glorious, sunlit evening. After we've let our dinner go down, we stroll to the beach. I'd intended to finally use my wetsuit today and have a dip in the North Atlantic Ocean, but the earlier cool winds and rain have put me off. We walk along the sandy beach in golden sunlight, barely needing a jumper. On the horizon, we can see Skye and even Kilt Rock, to add insult to injury. To the left, we see the mountains of Cuilin. To the right, in the far distance beyond Longa Island, is the light outline of Harris. Turning to walk back, I'm annoyed that I didn't have the nerve to try a swim. I know I'll regret not trying. This may be my only chance.

'I want to go for a swim,' I suddenly declare.

'Do you mean now?' James asks, with a slightly raised eyebrow.

'Yes, now.'

'I thought you'd started marching!'

We pick up the pace even more – the light is already beginning to fade. James wants to come back with me and bring the drone since it's a perfectly still evening. Ideal conditions for flying. And swimming. Hopefully. We race back to the van, where I quickly undress under the gazebo, knowing – and not really caring – that anyone looking will only get a moment's view, and squeeze into the wetsuit. I grab James's rock shoes (mine didn't seem to make it to Scotland) and my towel and start walking back to the beach. Typically, a large cloud has just hidden the almost-setting sun. James follows and takes a photo of me in my new suit before I enter the water. I grin.

I've always enjoyed running into the sea when I've had the opportunity. On previous holidays in Scotland, with a group of friends, a few of us started a tradition of running into the freezing water whatever the weather. Once, aged about 16, on the small Scottish island of Tiree, I ran into the sea in a bikini. I still remember the cold. Now, as I run towards the rippling waters, I try to prepare mentally for the shock of the low temperature. But this is something else. I knew before reaching the edge of the water that a wetsuit wasn't going to miraculously protect me from feeling the freezing temperatures, but as I get to waist height, I'm left breathless. I try to swim quickly to generate heat, but the water seeps in through a small gap in the collar, and I'm struggling to catch my breath. I try to laugh it off, but it's unnerving to feel I'm not getting enough air. I start shivering and swim back to shore.

James is still setting up the drone when I walk toward him, still soggy but instantly feeling warmer.

He looks at me and laughs. 'Is that it? Aren't you going back in?'

I take a breath. 'It's SO cold, James. I could hardly breathe!'

'You just need to get moving,' James suggests. 'Are you really not doing more than that?'

I know what he means, and I've got this far already. Now that I'm feeling warmer again, I do wonder if I should give it a second go. Leaving James, who's struggling to configure the drone, I head back in. To my surprise, while still bitterly cold, it doesn't feel so bad. I paddle about on the spot to get some warmth. As I do, I take a look around. The sun is peeking out from behind the cloud now. On shore, James finally has the drone in the air and is concentrating hard on controlling it. I turn and see mountains with sun-kissed tops. The sea stretches out, unbroken to the horizon, where it meets a bluish, golden sky. Then, faraway islands seem to rest on the very edge of the world. Shards of sun rays break through the cloud cover and reflect on the calm sea. It's almost silent, except for the tiny crashes of water around my shoulders and the distant sound of children on the campsite. Turned away from land, I am alone. Content. Happy to be alive in this intimate moment.

After a while, I feel the cold setting in once again, and I hear James powering down the drone. I swim toward the shore and run for my towel. I'd have loved a big, fluffy towel to encase my shivering body, but my microfibre half-size one will have to do. We climb back up through the dunes, where James stops to photograph the sunset. I continue to the site, heading straight for the showers after grabbing my pyjamas on the way. The water in the shower is hot. It feels like tiny daggers against my frozen skin, and I try to stay calm despite the scolding. The last thing we want is for me to faint on my own in this shower block.

The rest of the evening is a happy, relaxed one. We watch the Miami Qualifying on my iPad, tethering data from my phone, and get ready for bed. As we attach the blinds to the windows in the dusky light, I see other campers packing up chairs and tables and making their way inside their vans, tents and cars. Others are trying to round up children and get them to brush their teeth. Happy days.

11

DAY 7 – DO YOU RECOGNISE THIS MOUNTAIN?

We doze for a while after a really good sleep – probably the best we've had so far. It rains for half an hour or so. We were planning to get up and go quite early this morning, but we're both feeling slow and a little tired, so we have a cuppa and eat the porridge we bought from the site's shop. After being used to the same brand of porridge for a week now, the new porridge tastes odd. It's flavoured with frozen blueberries and bananas. It's not great.

It's a muggy morning, with insects hovering all around the van. Taking down the gazebo is an entertaining task, with mosquitoes and other bugs putting up a fight. I leave James to finish packing away while I walk to the showers, which takes me past caravans from which people are starting to stumble. I need to wash my hair, so I'm lugging all of my shower gear – shampoo, conditioner, hair gel, body wash. I even bring my razor, although I have no intention of shaving my legs. They're rivalling James's week-old beard, but I'm not exactly going to be in shorts anytime soon.

It feels so good to have clean hair again. I let it dry naturally rather than blast it into a big frizzy mess with the free hairdryer pinned to the wall.

Walking back to the car, the site is now busy with people milling around in the sunshine. I do my makeup in the car. My skin's looking a bit blotchy and spotty from dealing with layers of suncream, sprays of insect repellent and constantly touching my face to bat away bugs. I forgot to bring any concealer or foundation. Of course.

Today we're making our way to Ullapool, one of the places Nan visited on her Scotland trip. I flick through the pack of photographs from 21 years ago, and I'm excited at the thought of finally stepping into her shoes. Two of the photos have the inscription 'Firth by Ullapool' on the back, which isn't too helpful, but we'll try our best to locate them. They're of Nan and Aunty Hazel in front of a generic-looking loch and autumn-brown hills and mountains behind.

With everything packed away in the van, James starts the engine and trundles toward the reception area. We hop out and buy two takeaway coffees from the campsite's café before driving away, looking forward to getting back to the remote areas of these highlands. Initially, the drive takes us along the coast, and I watch the turquoise water gently ebb and flow against the yellow sand and dark rocks. I look over to James as he steers. The beard is really starting to fill in.

The smell of coconut fills the air from the plentiful gorse bushes that line the road. I feel like it might become the smell of the holiday. As the road twists and turns, I reflect on the past week and wonder how James is feeling.

'Is Scotland turning out to be better or worse than you expected? I ask.

'It's barmy!' James laughs, and after a quizzical look from me, he explains how the weather has made all the difference on certain campsites, how the constant travel has been more tiring than he thought and how the settings we've found ourselves in and the sights we've seen have blown his mind. What I don't realise is that as we excitedly talk over each other, thinking back over the last few days, I've accidentally opened my Notes app on my phone and pressed the record button, which types out our conversation. Or at least the snippets of each other's comments that it catches. The result, when I finally look down and see the paragraph I've created, is quite comical. Here it is:

It's what about you better than expected I was not expecting this weather that has made a massive this has been incredibly packed yet I think has we've been training is very wet. Misty can't really see the scenery and then trying to set up getting damp. I think I like along two weeks yeah but just I mean just you can see for miles that's what I maintain with camping camping. If the weather is good can best thing there is nothing better than camping oh I'm recording.

Technology can be the worst thing at times, but it can also – accidentally – be the best.

We pull over by Loch Ewe to admire the view along with other campers and motorhomers, with miles of water and peaks stretching out to our left and right. The sun is alone in the sky, and I want to bottle up this moment. Five minutes further into the journey, we pull over again to take a look at some seals basking in the light on rocks that protrude from the rippling water. I take photographs through the binoculars, creating circular images of seals in entertaining positions. After another few minutes, we drive past a family of mountain goats perched on a rocky mass overlooking the road, their curved horns contrasting against the jagged rock edges. We continue to search the sky for eagles. Every so often, we excitedly stop the car and zoom in through the binoculars, only to find that the 'eagle' we think we've spotted is a common buzzard. One time it won't be, though, we tell ourselves.

The road flattens out for a while, and we approach a group of cars parked on the right. It's not immediately clear what's attracted the attention of these people, but it's not long before we find out. We scan the miles of grassland to the right and spot two dark figures a way away. We pull over, adding Vera to the row of cars and vans currently occupying the layby. Through the binoculars, we watch two does nibbling at grass in the distance. No (live) stag yet, but what a lovely sight.

We carry on, towards Corrieshalloch Gorge and the Falls of Measah. There's a small car park off the road, which we pull into and make lunch – fried egg sandwiches. I've become quite desperate for a wee, so I run across the road and over a mound into a secluded grassy clearing. I find cover by some trees and do my first 'country wee' since leaving Birmingham. Go me.

We sit in the van and eat, careful not to spill egg yolk everywhere. A big sign in the parking area shows concept artwork for a new visitor centre with 'COMING SOON' plastered across it. It looks great – a shame we've arrived before its completion though. A path from the carpark leads through mossy woodland to a bridge over the falls. It's a very steep drop. My fear of heights is tested, especially when the bridge wobbles slightly as we walk across it. I hold onto the edge and peer over. James clasps my hand until we reach the other side. Walking a little further through the trees, a damp and earthy smell lingering in the air, we find the official viewing platform. It offers a beautiful view, but the drop to the bottom of the gap makes me feel funny, so I don't admire it for long.

Gorgeous moss covers the slopes between the trees to the sides of the path back to the car. I take a photo and send it to our friends Andy and Jo on our WhatsApp group chat. Jo loves a bit of moss.

As we drive around the corner, we suddenly spot a brand new, fully built visitor centre with a wealth of facilities – including toilets – and a café. Typical. And 'almost perfect' as usual. I'm tempted to write a strongly worded email to the owners about their inaccurate signage. I didn't need to have that country wee after all! I might leave that out of the email.

Approaching Ullapool, the sun dips behind a dark cloud, and the rain slowly falls. We park by Tesco and head out in our waterproofs. Ullapool seems like a lovely harbour town. We dive into an outdoors-based shop to wait for the rain to pass, checking out all the expensive camping gear we don't have and can't afford.

Towards the harbour, a small bookshop greets us on a corner. It's a quaint little shop with cards, postcards, novels, maps and some stationary. We choose an OS map as well as a postcard to send to my Mom. Walking toward the counter in the middle of the shop, I take out the two 'Firth by Ullapool' photographs from my pocket. Placing the map and postcard on the countertop, I present the photos and ask the friendly lady behind the till if she has any idea where they may have been taken. She's unsure.

'Might one of the mountains be Canisp?' She suggests. I thank her anyway for trying to help and explain the premise of our trip. 'What a lovely thing to do,' she remarks.

Turning to exit, I see a selection of magazines on a stand by the door, and I'm hit by the memory of Nan buying me Beano comics in my pre-teen years. My cousin Luke and I, who are four months apart in age, would always be treated to the latest Beano if Nan took us out to the shops. I had stacks of the comics over the years, most of which were purchased by Nan... I probably should have reimbursed her when I started earning money...

We leave the shop and walk down to the main harbour area. Frustratingly, maintenance works are taking place along the length of the street, with metal fencing and barriers blocking the view of the harbour. To make me feel better, we nip into a café nearby and have tea and ice cream. I ask the woman who serves us about the photos too. She takes the photos and holds them close to her face, almost touching her nose. She tells me that she's lived in Ullapool for 20 years, but she can't work them out either. 'That's going to annoy me all day,' she says with a frown.

Thankfully, the settings of the photographs of Nan in Ullapool itself are easy to locate. They were taken on the harbour's edge, just in front of the café we're in. Sadly, as we don our coats and step out of the door, I can't get to the water's edge because of the fencing. This is where Nan visited and stood. And I'm feet away. Almost perfect.

We get as close as we can to the spot where the photo of Nan was taken, and James holds up the image to line it up with what we see before us. James holds up his phone and takes a snap of the photograph in front of the view. It feels strange to know that I've finally 'found' Nan in a sense, but the moment is tinged with annoyance at the fact I can't stand on the shore, in the exact place she once stood, and picture her standing there, looking out at the boats and mist over the mountains. I take a minute to hold the photo and think of her. I miss her.

Satisfied we've seen as much of Ullapool as we need, we walk back to the van, past groups of tourists on walking tours. Continuing our journey north, the scenery is some of the most beautiful we've come across so far. I try to film a timelapse on my phone, propping it up on the dashboard. We drive for a few minutes, watching the road become narrower and narrower, cars having to give way at passing places to avoid accidents. I'm looking down at the photos of Nan in my hand, examining the shapes of the lochs and mountains, trying to decipher their locations, when I'm suddenly hurled forward, my head narrowly missing the dash. As quickly as the car dropped it rises again, and I'm thrown to the back of my seat. James pulls over.

'I'm so sorry – are you alright?' James asks, his hand on my arm as I catch my breath.

'What happened?' I ask, pressing my hand to my chest to check that my heart hasn't exited through my ribs. It's pounding.

'There was a huge motorhome veering into our side… I had to move over, and there was a massive pothole. Are you sure you're ok?'

I'm clutching the car door with my other hand, trying to calm down. I know I have some tablets in the back that I take when I experience shock, to prevent a panic attack, but I don't want to get them. I don't want to acknowledge that I'm in shock. If I can just calm down and act normal, I'll be fine. I ask James to keep driving. Tentatively, we trundle forward. Vera seems ok.

It's hot, again. The sun's out, and the car feels like an oven. This is not the Scotland we expected or were prepared for. I'm overdressed and starting to feel overheated. An hour or so later, and James is getting tired and feeling rough too. We still have 45 minutes left to go before we reach the next site, and it's a long, single-track road – if you can call it a road. It's a lumpy, bumpy ride. I don't get car sick usually, but we're both struggling as the car rises and falls over the uneven ground.

It's worth noting that, as with any great holiday, there are bound to be times that aren't as fantastic as others. And, as much as Scotland has so far produced many 'bottle moments', we were bound to meet with challenges at some point. Today is starting to feel that way. While our surroundings are stunning, the late-afternoon sun drenching everything in golden light, I just want to reach our next destination.

The track goes on and on. After a while, we stop taking in the view, eagerly hoping that the next corner will be the final one. The smell of coconut in the air is becoming less and less pleasant as the car lurches about with every dip and bump.

Eventually, we come to a decline that sweeps to the left, towards the sea and the Port A Bhaigh campsite. James pulls up and goes into the reception-slash-shop. I'm hot in the car but have no energy to move. There are two spaces available. We opt for the nearest one with an electric hook-up option. There's no signal on site, and the Wi-Fi is only available in the shower block. This isn't the best news when we were looking forward to finally relaxing this evening and streaming the Miami Grand Prix at 8:30 pm.

We try to eat some dinner, but we're feeling a bit sick and shaken up – literally and metaphorically – from the long, difficult drive and full day. We're presented with an idyllic view, but we barely take notice of it. I open the side door to get some air. Thankfully, it's starting to cool down. At 7:30 pm, we realise that the grand prix will start in an hour, and while it seems almost sacrilegious to choose to watch TV rather than soak up the coastal scenery, it's something we've been looking forward to all day. So we make a plan. After some exploration of the site, we work out that the Wi-Fi just about extends to about a metre outside the shower block. We take our camping chairs and my iPad and sit outside the chemical waste disposal area and the bins. Not exactly romantic, but the race streams perfectly. We sit in our jumpers and gradually start to feel better. Half-way through the race, a fellow camper, in a red t-shirt that's a little too small for him, walks past us and glances at what we're watching on the iPad.

'Miami?' he asks with a smile.

We nod and have a laugh with him. It's a good race. My fantasy Formula 1 team does well.

Once it finishes, we take ourselves back to the van and try to get some sleep. However, we have noisy neighbours who are badmouthing, loudly, the coronation and smoking weed, which wafts its way into the van. They quiet down at about midnight, mercifully. But just as soon as the talking stops, the rain begins. The sudden hammering of heavy raindrops on the metal roof wakes James with a start, which sends him into a panic. It's awful sensing him tense up, shuffling about and starting to shake. It's a state I've felt many times. I hold him and try to be positive. James prays. A real earnest, petitioning prayer for peace. No sooner have the words left his mouth when the anxiety seems to melt away. The realisation of an answered prayer is something truly incredible. He turns over and tries to drift off. The rain continues to beat against the van for most of the night. Neither of us sleep particularly well.

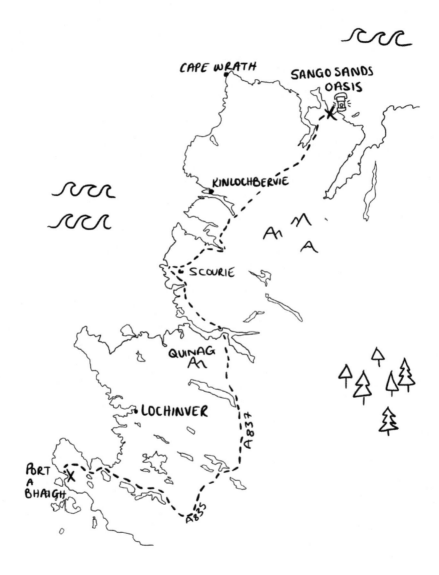

CAPE WRATH

SANGO SANDS
OASIS

KINLOCHBERVIE

SCOURIE

QUINAG

LOCHINVER

A 837

PORT
A
BHAIGH

A 8

12

DAY 8 – SCOTLAND SHOWING OFF

After the fairly eventful night last night, we both look a little worn out this morning. Again, we'd planned to head out earlier than usual to get on the road, but we can't hack it. So we slowly sit up and take down the blinds at the back of the van to appreciate the view. We did neglect it yesterday evening, so we try to take it in now. We're right on the coast, with jagged rocks and cliff edges falling into a gentle sea under the early sunlight. We can hear the mild hubbub of the site, with people packing up or making their way to the shower blocks.

James crawls out of the van to set up the Trangia for our morning tea and prepares the porridge pots. I'm still not sick of the porridge despite having had it every morning so far. I like routine, even if bland food is part of it. With some sustenance within, and feeling slightly more alert, we walk together towards the showers, towels and new clothes under our arms. Dark blue tiles encase the shower area, and the large mirror above the sinks is opaque with steam. I find an empty cubicle and slip on my trusty flip-flops. There's a bench opposite the shower head, on which I place my clothes and phone. The water spurts out of the shower head at more of an angle than I expected, so I reach and push my bundle of clothes further away to avoid a soggy outfit. The water is hot, and I take my time.

After packing up for the eighth time, we nip into the site's shop to stock up on more porridge, cereal, bread, milk, cheese and butter. We've also realised that we must have left our washing-up liquid at a previous site, so we buy some more. We have washing up to do from yesterday and this morning, so we take our new bottle of Fairy, careful to place it near the bowl so as not to forget it again, and wash up the bowls, cutlery, pan and cups. Eventually, at 11 am, we're ready to get going.

James drives to begin with, taking the same long, uneven road out of the site that we travelled down yesterday evening. It doesn't feel as horrendous this morning – maybe fresher eyes and knowing where we're heading today take the edge off each bump and jolt. The road, which for a while is nestled between peaks, starts to enter a bleaker, flatter landscape. It's not as dramatic as the mountainous areas we've driven through, nor is it green and lush. I can feel my heart starting to sink. Please let today be a brighter day. I want to have happy memories when I look back on this holiday. Soon though, we find ourselves passing Elphin, a little green gem of an area with rolling hills dotted with sheep, and I find the joy returning.

The landscape becomes increasingly dramatic as we near the northern coast, with snow-capped mountains and others that reach above the cloud layer. I keep an eye out for eagles, clutching the binoculars to be ready at a moment's notice.

I'm starting to need the loo, so at the hamlet of Kylesku, we pull over next to the tiniest public toilet block I've ever seen, with two toilets and no hand towels. The black tiles look moist, and I share the room with a far-too-high number of spiders.

It's lunchtime, so we wander down the road towards the Kylesku Hotel by the shoreline to check out the menu. Maybe we'll treat ourselves to a nice lunch with a view. But the menu is a celebration of seafood — and an expensive one at that. Not great for a vegetarian like me who doesn't eat fish. We agree to look elsewhere for food. At this point, I hop into the driver's seat to take over for the rest of the journey north. We cross a bridge and travel towards Scourie, home to a campsite and a Spar. The afternoon is rapidly disappearing, so I pop in to buy some crisps, and we make ourselves cheese sandwiches, which we eat in the car watching sparrows and wagtails dart about on the wall in front of us. It's like a show that's been put on just for us.

The drive from Scourie to Durness is incredible. If we were feeling flat at any point, those feelings soon melt away. We climb higher and higher on the side of hills until it feels like the cloud cover is just above our heads. The sun bursts through small cracks in the overcast sky, illuminating the rocky slopes of the giant peaks to our right, which reach high above the clouds. I keep my eyes on the road but occasionally turn to look out of my window, the view stretching on for miles and miles between the mountains. Living in a city like Birmingham, our eyes rarely get the chance to look at things further than a few metres away, so my eyes feel like they're getting some exercise. I take mental snapshots of the extraordinary scene.

The road narrows until it becomes only wide enough for one vehicle, so I have to make use of the numerous passing places. As we pass other drivers, it's noticeably clear who's local and who's just visiting. The locals drive at hilarious speeds and usually glare frustratingly at the big campervans and caravans blocking the route. I see one car heading my way, at a distance, and I don't have a passing place nearby. There'll be one for it to use, so I keep driving. But it doesn't stop, and I have to brake suddenly, finding the smallest of spaces on the edge of the road to let it through. I watch the driver race past. I receive the glare.

The wind picks up as we near Durness, and the trees all lean to one side. We see a sign for our site and soon turn in to the entrance to Sango Sands Caravan Park. It is gorgeous. Large, with lots of pitches, but plenty of space between each one and brand new facilities. We're assigned pitch 60, and I don't think we could have asked for better. As I approach the pitch, James jumps out to guide me in. I reverse so that we have a nice view out the back over the sea. As I look in my mirrors to check for James, I realise he has turned away from the van and is looking at the view and over the edge of the cliff. He turns around and smiles – an 'I-know-something-you-don't-know' smile – before calmly guiding me into the space and opening the door for me to get out.

'You've got to see this.'

As I step towards the end of our pitch and then peer over the small wooden fence, I'm greeted by a yellow, sandy shoreline and turquoise waves that gently crash against the dark rocks that jut out of the beach. The wind is behind us, so the van provides a barrier. We are warm in the sun. We stop for a few minutes and sit in silence, breathing in the view.

After slowly setting up the van for another night, folding down the bed slats, arranging the seat cushions and making the bed, we check out the facilities of the campsite. We listen to several conversations in different languages and accents. French, Yorkshire, Mancunian. As I use the toilets, I can hear James outside chatting to a man with a thick German accent.

There is a small café on the site, which sells hot food in the evening. Needing no further encouragement, we treat ourselves to pizza, chips and curry sauce and sit up to the table in the back of the van, watching people walk across the coastline in the golden light of a late-spring Scottish evening. I write up yesterday's escapades in my journal – I'm starting to get a little sloppy with keeping up with my journal, but I know I need to keep this record for future reference. My memory alone will never do this time justice.

Before the sun disappears, we decide to make the most of the dry, warm weather and head down to the bay below. There are two beaches on either side of a small peninsula that houses a viewing point at its end on which some of the campers are taking pictures. We opt for the furthest bay, which seems larger and is still mostly draped in sunlight. It's a steep walk down grassy and sandy dunes, and I wonder how easy it will be to clamber back up them.

'Golden' does not begin to describe the atmosphere of this bay. Not only is the light that gorgeous hue of a summer evening, but the wind has dropped, and the tide is slowly making its way inland. I watch as James walks away from me, weaving in between the black rocks that jut out from the sand. He clambers up a particularly jagged one and holds his arms out to either side, the breeze catching the sleeves of his navy jacket. When he hops down to ground level, we stroll across the sand, hand in hand, stopping to take photos that will never truly be able to capture this moment.

At one end of the bay are large, low, pink rocks. They seem out of place, so I Google what can create such a phenomenon. When searching 'pink rock Scotland', I shouldn't have been surprised to find search results for P!NK's future tour dates in Europe. Eventually, I ascertain that this is most likely pink granite. Apparently, pink granite is formed from an abundance of potassium feldspar. The milky speckles that decorate the stone are quartz. Black speckles are from amphibole and opaque ones from feldspar. Who knew?

The return climb up the dunes is entertaining. The sand slips away with every step, so it takes a sizeable number of strides to reach the walkway at the top again. We walk to the van and sit in the back with the doors wide open. As we sit sipping ginger tea, a man passes us on the path toward the beach but stops just in front of us to admire the view, his back to the van. We say nothing, allowing him to have this moment in a beautiful place. A couple approaches him and get talking to the individual, whose heavily accented voice reveals his Yorkshire background. They discuss the North Coast 500, their route, their vans, puffins. Puffins! At this point, I want to interject and ask where they've seen them, but I'm too shy to butt in. Plus, it's lovely to simply listen to people talking about their own journeys and what brought them here. They remain completely oblivious that we are feet away, listening to every word while sipping tea. Finally, they part ways. James and I giggle about inadvertently being flies on the wall.

The sun has well and truly dipped, so we put the table down and spread out the bedding, tucking the sheet around the corners of the seat cushions. The sky is partly clear and partly cloudy, so there's still a chance we could see the Northern Lights should there be any geomagnetic activity. James makes sure his phone is on loud to alert us in the night. I line up an episode of The Office on my phone, which we watch once we're locked in and tucked up.

We fall asleep quickly. I'm glad – even James seems calm, suggesting an anxiety-free night for both of us. But at 1:20 am I wake to thuds of rain beating down on the roof. Non-forecasted rain. Ten minutes later, James' phone pings with an alert. Possible aurora borealis visibility. I optimistically peek out of the water-streaked window. No chance.

NORTH ATLANTIC OCEAN

CAPE WRATH

DURNESS

A838

TONGUE

A836

BEN HOPE

NORTH
SEA

ORKNAY ISLANDS

THURSO

JOHN
O'GROATS

WICK •

13

DAY 9 – THE TOP (ISH) OF SCOTLAND

I can't believe we're on day NINE of our trip. We both feel as though we've got our mojo back after a brilliant day yesterday. A stunning morning follows what was a very wet night, as if the sun were saying 'What rain?'.

Despite the sunshine, I feel a tad grumpy. I don't know why. Maybe the daily travelling is getting to me. I want to get a good, positive start to the day so that we're not late getting to our next stop, but James – to me, at least – seems to be taking it slowly. I take a deep breath and get dressed. I grab my shower bag and towel and walk to the showers. But once I shut myself into a cubicle, I can't find my shower gel or my deodorant. This doesn't help the grumpiness. I shower as best as I can for a minute or so before the water seems to stop. Huffing, I keep pressing the metal button on the wall, but all I get is a trickle. It seems I came at the peak showering time, and I can hear the woman in the cubicle to my right pushing at her button, likely stealing my supply. I dry and dress, grumpier than before, and head back to the car. James gives me a big hug. We get going.

Many people told us before our trip that the north coast of Scotland doesn't have much to offer in the way of views. I wonder how they can say that, as I look out over the sea in one direction and over miles of open land toward greyed mountains in the distance in the other. We drive in near silence for about 15 minutes, scanning the landscape for deer or eagles when I think I spot something.

'Probably just a buzzard,' James suggests.

'I know, but one day it might not be – it looks huge anyway!'

James pulls the van over and grabs the binoculars, holding them to his eyes and leaning out of his window.

'You're right – it is big.'

We're far away from the bird, but it's clearly no buzzard. There is a lighter part on its wings, and, again, it's massive. I check out James's bird guide app, and we try to take clear photos through the binoculars. It is. It really is. A young golden eagle. It lands on a rocky outcrop and then flies off, gliding between the hills and giving us a great view. We're so excited.

'We can go home now,' I joke. The photos are a little grainy, so we don't have great evidence to back up our claims, but we know we've seen it. And it's so exciting. I mentally 'tick' off one of our bucket list items for the trip.

After all the excitement, we travel on until we reach the small town of Bettyhill, where we stop at a café. It's a lovely wood-panelled building, where the walls are lined with bottles, artwork and hand-crafted items, with friendly staff and great toasties. We take a round table in the corner, by the window. It's nice to stop and listen to the locals while being warmed by the sunlight beaming through the glass. We buy two brownies to go, and as we're paying, we get chatting with the bar woman, who explains that they're much busier now than they were at this time last year.

'It must quiet down later in the year – when it gets cold?' asks James.

'Aye, but not completely. We had visitors doing the 500 at Christmas,' she explains.

'We're not that hardcore,' I laugh.

'Neither am I. And most were in tents!'

I shudder at the thought.

With brownies safely stored in takeaway boxes, we continue our drive along the north coast. A sea mist gradually obscures the view, becoming thicker and thicker until we struggle to see much of our surroundings at all. What we do notice though, is the land levelling out. The mighty peaks are behind us, making way for vast, flat farmland. We see countless square fields of sheep, cows, pig – even rheas, a relative of the ostrich. The landscape is not as dramatic as we've seen, but certainly full of life.

The road winds along until we see signs pointing toward John O'Groats, often thought to be the most northerly point of the UK. In actual fact, Dunnet Head is the most northerly point of the UK mainland, 2.35 miles further north than John O'Groats. Our next campsite is actually before the landmark, but to save time tomorrow, we decide to visit the famous sign today and then double back on ourselves to come to the site. If we're honest, visiting John O'Groats wouldn't be something on our list to do if this were a normal holiday. But Nan went there, and so must we.

Considering that it's such a famous part of the country and a tourist hotspot, we're surprised by how quiet and… underwhelming… it is. As we pull into the car park, James says he expected to have to walk a little way along the shore to reach the sign. Instead, we catch sight of the white signpost before we've even parked up. There's a small group of bikers in leather jackets near the sign, but other than that, no one seems to notice it. Have we come on a weird day? Is a Tuesday not the day for tourists? As we stroll toward the sign, James asks one of the jacketed bikers to take a photo of us, who kindly agrees. We stand on either side of the sign and lean on the pole, trying to avoid the small puddle at its base. 'Cheese!'.

Nan came on a bright, sunny day. We've got clouds. When I spoke to Aunty Hazel before the trip, I asked her if there were any funny moments she remembered from her holiday with Nan. One in particular was during their visit to John O'Groats. She told me that when they visited the sign, they met a young man on a bicycle and got chatting with him. Where was he from? Birmingham. Here, about 550 miles from home, who should they meet? Of course, a fellow Brummie. She told me that they laughed about the coincidence. In one of the photos we found of Nan's trip, there is a bald man in a bright yellow jacket, standing with his bicycle in front of the sign. The date on the sign is September 18th, 2002. I wonder where that man is now. Mom also found a postcard from Nan, addressed to us, from this very day too. In full, it reads,

Dear Fiona & Rosie,

We are really here, looking across the sea to the Orkney isles. The sun is shining

& it is quite warm. We have been to the Gunn Museum & had lunch in Wick. Very tempted to take the ferry to the isles!!

Missing you,

Lots of love,

From Mom (Nan) & auntie Hazel.

I take a moment to picture Nan here. I have no photos of her with the sign. The only evidence that Nan came here lies in the postcard she sent and the blurred edge of a finger on a photo of Auntie Hazel in front of a gift shop that seems to have disappeared at some point in the last 20 years. I can imagine her short hair and long pleated skirt gently blowing in the breeze.

As you should always do at popular attractions, we head into the current gift shop. Among the 'tat', as we call it, I spy a little book on the Gunn clan, similar to Nan's. Perhaps this is where she bought her own little book on the clan, which I remember always being on her bedroom bookcase at home. I buy it. Having seen all we want of John O'Groats, we hop back in the car and take the short drive back along the road to the Ferry View Night Stop.

'Quirky' is one word for it. On arrival, we are greeted by a large red bus to the right of the entrance and a multi-coloured wooden shed that acts as a reception. We meet Nikki, who co-runs the site. She is very friendly and helpful and directs us to Pitch 3. Driving through the small site, we pass gnomes, bunting, sparkly ornaments… We glance at each other and stifle a laugh. There are only six pitches, so it isn't long before we find ours. We drive straight in, ensuring the back doors open to a sea view. Well, almost… a row of trees obscures the scene, but it is still miles better than our usual view from our flat back in Birmingham. We walk up through the small site to the reception block, where Nikki takes payment for our stay and shows us the facilities. The two shower rooms use timed slots, morning and evening, allowing for thorough cleaning between uses. This sounds great – we've been used to wearing our flip-flops in every site's shower and trying to find dry cubicles for over a week now. However, it does mean that we're limited as to when we can get in them in the morning. We think we might have an early departure in the morning, so we consider booking an evening slot, but we need to properly plan the day. We agree to let Nikki know which slot we'd like later. The site handily has a washing machine too, so we empty our bag of washing into the drum and walk back to Vera.

I set up the table and bench seats in the back while James hunts for the OS map and the brownies we bought earlier. Once we're sat with brownies in hand, we spread the map out on the table, focusing on the section of Scotland we plan to cover tomorrow. There are a lot of areas coming up that are not only on Nan's handwritten list but are also shown in the pack of photographs Mom found of Nan's trip. Many we'll be passing on the next leg of our journey, so we need to decide what we can reasonably spend time visiting.

The most important to me is the Gunn Museum. We already know it will be closed, but there is a wonderful photo of Nan standing in front of the sign at the entrance of the building. I want to stand where she stood. Other places that are on the route are Tain ('tea on way North'), Dingwall, Loch Ness, Alcaig and Inverness. Looking at the map, we can likely manage all apart from Inverness in one day. Considering where we're staying tomorrow, we can squeeze Inverness into the following day. Other areas mentioned on the list or shown in photos include Cromarty Firth and Fort George. They are a little out of the way to manage to reach them in 24 hours, and I have no photos of Nan at either place, so we agree to wave at them from afar but focus on the places in which I can really picture her.

A growing rumbling sound appears to come from the site's entrance, so we poke our heads out of the back of the van. A colossal motorhome is trundling its way down the site, with an older couple looking a little nervous in the cabin. We watch as they edge their way past our van. And we wince as the man elects to perform a three-point turn in a space in which even we would have found tricky to manoeuvre. James is literally on the edge of his seat as we witness the rear wheels of this motorhome reverse onto and over the top of a wooden border, causing the shiny white rear to back into, bend and break a young sapling. Nikki and her partner, Royston, come running toward the scene from the reception, and we hop out of the car to offer help. The rear wheels are now lodged in grassy mud behind the wooden beam that's set in the ground, so Royston runs away to retrieve some planks to set under the wheels and try to provide some grip. A few minutes later, all four wheels are in the central pathway, and the motorhome is gently steered into its assigned pitch. And, breathe.

After all the commotion, we decide to book a shower slot, but when we check in with Nikki again, the only times available are between 7 and 8 am and 10 and 11 am. Bright and early it is then. It will be good to have the motivation to get a good start to the busy day planned for tomorrow.

As dinner time approaches, we order food on the amazing old red and blue bus that Nikki and her partner Royston have transformed into a sweet little restaurant, equipped with four round tables with two chairs each and a section at the rear presenting locally made arts and crafts. I order a falafel burger, and James an Angus beef burger with chips. While we wait, two bikers and the couple who not long ago arrived in the enormous, rented motorhome take seats on the bus with us. At least one of the bikers is from Wigan. We learn this when he explains that they've ordered pizzas here before, which are, apparently, amazing.

'Everyone in Wigan knows about these pizzas,' he declares.

Shame I didn't know that before placing my order. The couple in the motorhome are from Surrey. They flew to Edinburgh and hired their vehicle.

'That's cheating!' We joke. Everyone chuckles.

For about 20 minutes, we chat with each other about all sorts of things. The sun is gloriously shining through the large windows of the bus, and the temperature is rising. I can feel my right arm, bare beyond my t-shirt sleeve, starting to catch the sun. Even James starts to look a tad flustered. So when our food comes, we say our goodbyes and take it back to the van to eat at our table, looking out of the windows at the various fairies dotted around the grounds.

The light gradually diminishes, and the almost-clear sky means another chance to see the Northern Lights. James makes sure his phone is set to loud again to alert us of any possible sightings. I set my alarm for 7 am.

It doesn't rain in the night. It's a perfect opportunity to see the

Northern Lights. And it may be one of the last chances we'll get, with the weather looking to take a turn from tomorrow.

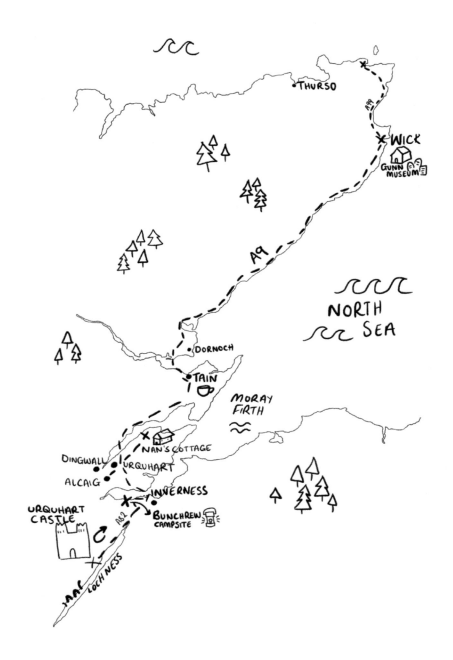

14

DAY 10 – DOREEN BANKS WAS HERE

The loud alarm echoes around the van at 7 am, and we're pleased to find that we both slept well. Yet, we realise that there was no aurora alert during the night. Gutted. Oh well. We'll just have to come back.

It's a chilly morning, but we feel snug under our duvet, so the last thing I want to do is drag myself out into the cold. But we need to be showered and out of our assigned bathroom by 8. James goes first to give me time to rally some energy, and I follow. I forget my shower flip flops, but then remember that, for the first time, I don't feel that I really need them. 'Bathroom 1', as it's named on the laminated sign blu-tacked to the door, is clean, light and even marginally warm. The shower is in the corner, with sparkly black tiles on the walls and shining glass doors. A step up from some of the cobwebbed and chilly showers we've experienced.

Back at the van, we pack up and quietly drive out of our pitch and toward the entrance, trying not to disturb the other campers. I'm sure the couple from Surrey won't hear a thing, tucked up in their motorhome bedroom, but the bikers are in small green tents, and I hope we leave them snoozing. The quirky site continues to surprise us. Nikki meets us to retrieve the keys for Bathroom 1, and she explains that we can order breakfast to go. Yes please. Two teas, poured into our travel mugs to prevent waste, pancakes (for me) and a breakfast burger (for James) are soon in our possession. It's a delicious start to the day. I don't miss my usual porridge one bit. The tea is Yorkshire tea, with the perfect amount of milk to produce a good 'builder's tea'. It feels good to be getting on the road so early. There's much to do today.

The mist is in, so it's not the most scenic of drives as we begin our journey south, but it is atmospheric. We pass numerous farms with lots of different livestock. Then, there's a large wind farm, but only the bottom halves of the turbines are visible, and they stretch high into the thickening cloud cover.

Our first stop is Latheron, home to the Gunn Museum. I know how excited Nan was to visit it, and I can feel anticipation building in my stomach. I'm glad I've prepared myself already for the fact that it will be closed. But my hope is that we can still walk around the building and see the exact spot where Nan posed for a photo. In 45 minutes, we enter the small town of Latheron, looking for signs pointing to the museum. Finally, we make a turn onto a short lane that leads to the building. The mist – probably now classing as fog – has increased, which makes the slow roll down to the museum very eerie. As we approach, I realise that it is a former church building, surrounded by numerous gravestones, some of which are standing, but most are laid flat. The weathered white building looms out of the fog, and I'm glad to see that the black gate at the front of the property is open. I was prepared to hop the gate if the need arose, but my law-abiding nature takes a sigh of relief. I grab the relevant photos from the envelope, and we make our way, hand in hand, through the gate.

I'm nervous and excited. This feels like the first proper 'finding Nan' moment of the trip. I spot the big sign on the front of the building, I take out the photo of Nan and hold it up, lining it up with the edges of the building. And there she is. My Nan. Proudly posing for a picture taken by her sister in front of this little museum, her hands together holding a strap of her handbag and a pair of glasses. I take a deep breath of the cool, damp air and slowly release it. A small cloud emerges before me as I exhale. A tear – or two – trickles down my cheek.

On closer inspection, I realise that the sign, although similar to the one in Nan's photo, has changed, and, in my personal opinion, not for the better. From afar, you can see 'THE CLAN GUNN HERITAGE CENTRE' in large print, followed by a highly misleading giant, bold, black 'OPEN' on a stark white background. Below this, in small print, are the details of open times – June to September, Monday to Saturday, 11:00 am to 4:00 pm. James asks me to stand in front of the sign, and he takes a photo. I hold up the picture of Nan, and he takes another one. I hope Nan won't mind that my hair is in space buns today – she was always so refined and put together; she didn't always care for 'scraped-back' hair as she put it. She can tell me off when I see her again.

It is cold. We do a quick lap of the building and peer into the windows. Inside, there are photographs and paintings on the walls, but the tables and shelves are either empty or strewn messily with books or fabric. I'm surprised at the state of the interior, given that the museum is due to open in three weeks.

As we walk around the perimeter, trying to avoid stepping on graves, we read some of the names on the headstones. Ironically, I don't see many Gunns. I do spot a few Mackenzies, which is funny because the surname appears in James's ancestry. Did our long-lost relatives know each other perhaps? It's unlikely, given that both surnames aren't particularly uncommon, but we still laugh at the coincidence. The paving stones – which, on reflection, may well have been worn graves – are slippery from the mist, and more than once we both lose our step. Carefully, we circle back to the car. I take one final look at the building, which is almost disappearing in the grey-white fog, and feel the tears brimming once again.

Like a robot, I sit in the passenger seat and pull my seatbelt across, staring in front of me as I click it into place. I feel James take my hand and give it a light squeeze. I feel ecstatic, emotional, numb… I don't really know. The engine turns over, and we trundle toward our next stop: Tain. Composing myself, I look at the handwritten list of Nan's on my phone. Next to 'Tain', Nan wrote 'Tea on way north'. So we're going to go for tea on our way south. The fog is thick now, and James drives steadily. Thankfully, the road is in much better condition compared to what we've experienced over the past 10 days, so we're not caught out by any surprise potholes.

Eventually, we see signs for Tain. It's a little town, and we park for free in the town centre. A good sign – anywhere that offers free parking in the middle of its busiest area suggests it's a nice place to me. We know our mission here: to have a cuppa. We stroll around the corner from the car park, looking for a café or something similar. We pass a gorgeous building that holds a restaurant called Greens. It looks a bit posh, but in the gloomy atmosphere, it also feels warm and inviting, so we peek inside. Behind the large glass windows are wooden tables and comfy chairs, mostly occupied by locals. There's a small sofa and short round table in a corner, currently vacant, so we take a seat and order two teas and a delicious-sounding pear and cinnamon scone to share.

Perfect. At first, the Scottish lady who serves us gives off a certain vibe that makes us think she doesn't really like us. Is it our accents? She appears to ignore our compliments about the place. Perhaps she just didn't hear us. The next time she passes, we try again, expressing our delight at the gorgeous scones they offer.

'We like to do unusual scones every day – banana and chocolate, things like that,' she says with a smile.

Sounds heavenly. Full of tea and scone, we leave the restaurant and trot down the road, admiring the mixture of grey and yellowing stone buildings. There are signs for the Tain Golf Club, a bowling green, a company called North Coast Glass and a nearby coastal walk route. Tain is quiet, and I like it. I think Nan must have liked it too. It's doubtful she had her tea in the building that we just did, but I can imagine her and her sister strolling through this old town.

Onwards. We pull over in Dingwall, where we pick up some lunch and continue right through to Alcaig, where Nan stayed in a bungalow. We have photos of the bungalow, but only a vague description written on the back of one of them, which says 'Bungalow at Alcaig'. Looking at Google

Maps, Alcaig appears to be a relatively tiny area, so, in theory, we have a decent chance of finding it.

Alcaig seems to comprise a small collection of houses – some holiday lets, others local homes. From the photo, the bungalow Nan stayed at was right by the water, so we're able to quickly discard many of the buildings we pass on our route through the area. The small road we decide to take leads to a dead end, so we turn around. In almost no time, we've scoured the whole of Alcaig. I'm disappointed, but I'm not too surprised. Nan's grasp of directions was never wonderful, and after more than 20 years, the bungalow may well have changed or not even exist anymore.

Thinking about Nan's geography skills, I recheck the map. A little further up the road is a similarly small area, called Urquhart. I can see that the road through Urquhart winds down toward the water and along the firth, and some buildings are unmarked. What do we have to lose from trying? In a last-ditch attempt to find the bungalow, we drive to the top of the road we're on in Alcaig and take a left, slowly travelling down the small lane. I eagerly scan every roof, wall and gate I see.

I can see on Google Maps that we're nearing the end of the track, and I begin to brace myself for another disappointment. However, as the water to our left creeps closer to the path, I spot a familiar-looking brown roof peering over some bushes on our right. As we pass the bushes, I spy a low-walled entryway that leads to a bungalow. *The* bungalow. A couple are sitting in the paved area outside the front of the bungalow enjoying a drink, so we pull over a few metres past the entrance, out of sight.

I can't believe it. We found it – the 'bungalow in Alcaig' that's not even in Alcaig! I don't know what to do. I'm squealing internally and perhaps accidentally externally because James reaches over and grasps my hand once again.

I collect the photos of the bungalow, which sadly don't include Nan but do show the building at several angles, highlighted in evening sunlight. We exit the van, and I awkwardly walk up to the reclining couple.

'I'm so sorry to bother you', I stammer, 'and this is a bit random, but my Nan stayed here 20 years ago, and –' I'm cut off by a voice to my right.

'Can I help you?'

A dark-haired woman in her late 60s has appeared from the side of the bungalow, paint brush in hand. The couple explain that they are only stopping here; this woman owns the property. I turn to this paint-brush–yielding woman and repeat what I said to the couple, who seem a little puzzled as to what's taking place in front of them.

'I'm so sorry to bother you, but we're taking a trip around Scotland visiting places that my Nan went to over 20 years ago. She stayed here with her sister... Would you mind if I took some pictures? She passed away three years ago.'

'That's fine,' paint brush woman says. 'What was her name?'

'Doreen Banks,' I say, finishing with a smile as I think about all the people who have said her name wrong over the years. It's Duh-reen, not Door-reen. It was one of the banes of her life.

Paint brush lady turns her head as if she can almost picture Nan, but then she tells us that this couple, pointing to the two now standing nearby with drinks in hand, also came here 20 years ago.

'We came in 2002,' the man explains.

'That's the same year as my Nan!' I reply. What are the chances?

It starts spitting with rain before I can ask any more of the questions I had in mind. In what month did the couple visit in 2002? Does paint brush lady have a record of Nan and her sister staying? Or even a guestbook they wrote in? They all head inside, and I don't have the nerve to ask if I can peek inside too to compare it to the photos. Instead, I stand back and line up Nan's photos against the real-life scene in front of me, trying to capture the pictures before the raindrops distort the images. Suddenly, the rain gets heavier, so we run back to the car for cover, flopping into our seats and slamming the doors behind us. We did it. We found the unfindable bungalow. Almost perfect, were it not for the rain. I close my eyes and smile. I feel James squeeze my hand again.

There's little time to pause. Next is Loch Ness. There are two sweet photos in the envelope, clearly taken by Auntie Hazel, of Nan leaning over a wall, with binoculars against her eyes, looking out over the loch. James studies another photo taken on the same day, which shows Urquhart castle, on the shore of Loch Ness, so that's where we head.

As we approach the famous tourist attraction, we pass countless gift shops filled with your classic, stereotypical Scottish memorabilia. Tartan everything. Pens, hats, bookmarks, scarves. While the rain had petered out on the short drive, it begins to fall again as we enter the car park on the side of the loch. I immediately see where the photos were taken 21 years ago: on a strip of walkway that is currently blocked off by metal fencing.

Typical. We're not planning on staying long; I visited Loch Ness on a group trip in my mid-teens, and James has no desire to search for Nessie. We park in a bay close to where I think Nan stood, and I pull my hood over my head as I step out of the van. The photos are in my pocket to protect them from the rain. I try to locate exactly where Auntie Hazel had been when she captured Nan at that moment. Sadly, the viewing point that Nan looked out from is now blocked by the metal fence, and the wall is drastically overgrown. There's no way to lean on the wall and get a good look at the loch like Nan did. It's a shame, but I'm able to position myself to almost get Auntie Hazel's view. The rain is now pouring down, so I quickly take out the photo to capture the memory. Auntie Hazel's photo, I appreciate as I examine it again, is actually quite beautiful. It catches such a candid moment. We only see part of Nan's face. She isn't posing. She's just enjoying looking through her binoculars at this famous loch while holidaying with her sister.

Water is now running off the rim of my hood, so we run back to the car and laugh as we drive off without paying a penny to the probably very rich management company of the tourist attraction. However, we don't leave without stopping near a gift shop in the nearby town and picking up a novelty pen for Laura. James and Laura have a tradition whenever they go on holiday.

Years ago, before I even entered the scene, James and his sister had decided that rather than spending valuable time in and out of shops looking for the perfect gift while away, they would instead buy a pen that had some bearing on the holiday – a useful (yet fun) gift, and one that is fairly easy to come by. The first James remembers gifting Laura was a baguette-shaped pen from France.

So, as we scan the shelves and display tables, it isn't long before James spots the perfect gift. The pen in question is mostly white, with 'Scotland' written on the side and a tiny green figurine of the Loch Ness Monster dangling from a short chain at the top of the pen. Wearing a tartan hat.

It's been a big day. We gently make our way to our next site, Bunchrew. It's not far from Inverness, where we'll visit tomorrow, and is an attractive, open site, with plenty of space between pitches. The rain has been coming and going all day, so when we park up on our pitch on the outer ring of the spiral-shaped site, we elect to put the gazebo up to prevent a sleepless night. We've still got packets of curried grains and spiced rice, so we opt to use some leftover bread and heat up a couple of packets, producing two hearty grain-filled bowls of goodness. A middle-aged couple are in the space next to us. They have a larger van, which they've converted into a camper, plus a whole tent that they've attached to the side. At one point, the man walks past the end of our gazebo while we're sitting in the back with a cuppa. He peers in and compliments the van.

'Doesn't matter what size you're working with, does it?' He says, before explaining that he and his 'missus' come to the site about six times a year. Six!

We've accumulated a large amount of clothes that need washing, so we make the most of the facilities. Walking behind our van and along a narrow, damp, grassy path between caravans, I find an old stone building that houses a couple of washing machines and tumble dryers. I start with the washing machines, returning after they've finished to load the freshly washed clothes into one of the big dryers. With the weather so intermittent, I decide the risk of shrinking clothes is worth it.

Thankfully, all our clothing remains the size they're intended to be when I collect it. By the time we've eaten and got into bed, the clouds have parted, and it's another clear evening, so we again set James' phone on loud to alert us for any possible sighting of the Northern Lights. That would be the cherry on top for today.

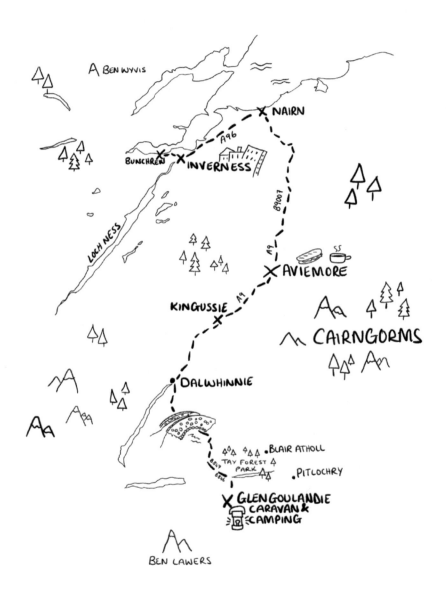

15

DAY 11 – A 'LOVELY' SEASIDE TOWN

No aurora alert during the night, again. I'm feeling dozy when we sit up in bed and open the blinds to look at the scenery. It's not the best view we've had on this trip, but it certainly beats that of our home in Birmingham. We're set back from the water's edge – that of Beauly Firth – and other campervans dot the site between us and the water.

It's a still morning and more overcast than we expected. James is particularly sleepy, so I crawl out of the van to brew up a cup of tea. It's quiet on the site; few seem to be up and about, and those who are awake appear to be quietly getting on with their morning routines. I pass James his mug as I creep back under the duvet.

'Not much more left', James says.

It takes me a moment to realise that he's referring to the length of our trip. I pout. When he finishes his tea, James heads to the shower while I start putting things together to prepare to pack up for the day. There are only two places on Nan's list to visit today, so we can take things at a gentler pace than yesterday.

I'm so slow this morning that James comes back from his shower before I'm even half-way through sorting things out. I'm glad of the timing, though; James looks frazzled as he walks towards me, towel slung over his shoulder.

'Have you been in the shower yet?' He asks.

'No; sorry, I'm being slow this morning. You ok?'

'Just about – the shower was *screaming* hot. I couldn't stand under it for long', James explains. 'Be careful; you know what you're like…'

He's not wrong. I've fainted more than once when it's been a hot, sunny day, and if I feel overly warm in a room or vehicle where I can't get near a window or an open door, I instantly start to panic. So as I grab my towel and flip-flops, I ready myself for a challenge. The facilities on this campsite are nice and clean, if a little dark. I enter a shower cubicle and see that it operates a chain pulley system. Old school. I like it. There isn't much space in the cubicle, so when I'm ready, I stand as far away from where I expect the spray to reach and stretch to pull on the chain.

How anyone could have a proper shower with this water is beyond me. I'd contemplated washing my hair today. But there's no way I'm putting my head under this steaming, molten flow. I do my best to wash before having to call it a day. Ironically, I feel slightly chilly due to standing at just enough of a distance away from the main target area of the shower head. I dress quickly and squelch my way back to the van in my flip-flops.

After packing up Vera, we hop into the front and make our way to another of Nan's listed locations: Inverness. It's not somewhere we'd have chosen to visit had this just been a normal holiday. When Nan went, she took photos of the town, and I'm interested to see how those shops have changed in 21 years. We drive for just 13 minutes before arriving and parking in a small car park near Eastgate.

I managed to find the location of the photographs last night. In one of the images, there's a rather grand-looking building with 'Royal Bank of Scotland' in large, block white letters attached to the front. Even if all the other shops have changed names over two decades, surely that's remained? When I search for this bank on Google Maps, I do find it, but it's now further down the road from the original stately edifice, in a smaller, house-like building. I wonder when it got the downgrade. I'll have to research that later.

It's a misty, drizzly walk to the town centre, and the weather clearly doesn't care about my mission to photograph my Nan's pictures out in the open. Hoods up, we walk down some steps onto Eastgate and immediately look down the same street that my Nan and Aunty Hazel did in 2002. I have the photos in my waterproof coat's pocket to keep them safe and dry until I find the perfect spot. We walk a little further down the road until I think we've found it. I take out the photos and find the one that matches my view. With one eye closed, I try to line up the first photo as best I can. The right-hand side matches perfectly, so I use my other hand to take photos with my phone.

The funniest thing I notice is that there is still a Clarks in exactly the same place. The bank may have had a downgrade, but, apparently, Clarks hasn't lost its audience here. I register a difference: Burton Menswear is now Slaters. No grand changes on this street, then.

Walking further down the road, I spot the building that once held the Bank of Scotland and find the photo in my pocket. It's now the home of the Caledonian, a standard family-friendly pub that's rated 3.8 stars out of 5 on Google. In Nan's photographs, it shows a Woolworths, one of Nan's favourite shops and one that James and I both miss (mostly because of the Pick-n-Mix), standing next door. There's now a Poundland in its place. To the left of the Caledonian is House of Highlands, a clothing shop full of every stereotypically Scottish item of clothing you could need: kilts, scarves, sporrans... I reckon Nan would have loved it. She'd have enjoyed finding all the references to the Gunn Clan. In one of Nan's photos, she stood in front of what I can only presume was a bakery with the name 'Bakers Oven'. Sadly, it's now another clothing store.

The third and final Inverness-based photo of Nan's is of another grand structure, which I initially thought to be a large church, opposite the Caledonian. Comparing the photo with what I see before me, I wouldn't believe that any time has passed. Apart from there not being a bagpipe player between myself and the building, it looks identical. It won't be until I get home and start drafting this book that I consider looking up the building online to find out about it. It's no church. It's the Inverness Town House. A listed building, it was constructed in 1882 by William Lawrie in the Gothic style and officially opened in the same year by the then Duke of Edinburgh, Prince Albert, son of Queen Victoria.

Happy that we've found each of the Inverness-based locations photographed by Nan, we decide to circle back to the van. The rain is, yet again, starting to get heavier as we walk along the same street back toward Vera. We're approached by a young woman on the way, clearly unbothered by the rain, who wants to talk to us about homelessness. We apologise that we can't talk, and she cheerily wishes us well. There's clearly a homelessness issue in this area; we pass more than one shop front that advertises support groups and charities seeking to help individuals dealing with this challenge.

Back in the van, I use Google Maps to direct us to the final specific town that I know Nan visited: Nairn. In her list, she makes a sweet little note to say that this next stop is a 'lovely seaside town along [the] coast from Inverness'. Although it's still overcast and a tad damp, I'm looking forward to seeing this place.

Our initial reaction as we roll into Nairn is... underwhelmed. We don't find it to be a 'lovely' area; it feels achromatic and mildly bleak. Maybe it's the weather. The cloud covering doesn't highlight any beauty in the mostly grey buildings that we pass, and there aren't many people milling about. We park by the library and walk around the block to see if it improves when investigated on foot. It's cold, so we briskly walk through the shop-lined streets, but it's not too inviting. Soon enough we're at the van again, contemplating what to do.

'Shall we just drive down to the beach', I suggest, 'to see if it's better down there?'

It doesn't get better. I drive us down to the water's edge, where there's no parking unless you want to visit the Leisure Centre, which we don't fancy. There is a green area with a bandstand in the middle and lots of benches, which I can imagine being filled with happy families on a warm, sunny day, but it's deserted today, and the misty drizzle gives it an eerie feel.

We both agree that over 20 years ago, this could well have been a bustling, happy town with lots of busy shops and local attractions. But now, there's a huge caravan park taking up much of the area by the shore, and few seem to be visiting. It's a shame not to feel the same way as Nan about this area, but I guess that's what time does to places. They can be popular destinations for a period of time before losing the visitors to other areas that have new, exciting features.

The plan had been to grab some lunch in Nairn, but with nowhere that jumps out at us, we choose to get on our way toward our next campsite, Glengoulandie, and I pick up the driving. I'm excited about this stop. It was one of the last places we booked as we were deciding how to plan the last leg of the trip. The owners were super friendly in their email correspondence, and I've requested pitch 12, in a corner of the site that has great views.

On the way, we stop at Aviemore for lunch. An unusual, busy little place with a real mix of shops and eateries. We eventually settle on a small café, choosing window seats and those high stools you get when you sit up to a kitchen island or bar. We order baguettes and watch the world go by. While sipping my drink, I notice that there's a nice shop next door that sells soaps, body washes… that kind of thing.

'Let's just pop in there before we go,' I say, nodding toward the shop sign that's visible out the window.

In the shop, we smell so many fragrances that after a few minutes, I'm not sure what anything smells like anymore, but I select a gorgeous tweed gift bag that contains hand cream and body lotion that smell lovely – at least I think they do. I hope my friend Jo likes the scent. She'll be having her baby in just a few weeks, so I want to treat her to something nice.

A little way up the road, we nip into another shop, and I buy a tin of loose-leaf 'highland tea' for Mom while James buys a pencil with a highland cow stuck on top for Laura.

What began as drizzle soon becomes a heavy shower as we race back to the van, weaving through tourists and locals. We stomp through shallow puddles and splash our way through the carpark, rushing to open the car doors. We take a breath as we put our seatbelts on and then get back on the road, travelling South.

En route, we drive through a town called Kingussie, which I visited with a large group about 14 years ago. James pulls over so that I can take a quick selfie with the sign welcoming visitors to the town. I send the photo to some who were in the group. I was just 14 when we went, and I have many happy memories of that holiday.

As we near Glengoulandie, we turn off the main road onto yet another single-track road that, at first glance, doesn't appear to lead anywhere in particular, but we trust Google Maps. Our first hurdle is a small stone bridge over a brook that has a 'Road Closed' sign next to it. It's not blocking access but, clearly, works are underway here… albeit not right now. Another sign next to it explains that work will proceed from May 8, 2023, and last five months. So, work supposedly started three days ago.

But there's no sign of this on the bridge itself. The only indication that something's going on is the sight of a van and a car on the other side of the brook near a small section of metal fencing. James drives forward.

'What are you doing?' I shriek. I like rules. Especially following them. 'The sign says we can't go over the bridge!'

'It'll be fine – they haven't done anything to it yet…' James justifies as he begins to approach the stone structure.

'It's going to collapse – or something. Oh–'

Before I can even finish my worried thought, we're over the other side.

'See?'

I'm still gripping the seat. 'Can you check with those guys if we can drive this bit?' I ask as we approach to two vehicles, where two men are clearly about to head home.

I wind my window down as we pull up to the rear of the parked car so that James can speak to them, but as he's trying to get their attention, the man in the car we're blocking simply honks his horn in a 'get-out-of-my-way-I-want-to-go-home' kind of way.

We take that as an indication to carry on. The road winds and weaves its way through the hills, past shrubs and brownish heather. For 20 minutes or so, we quietly enjoy the undulating terrain, watching buzzards soar high overhead, ready to grab the binoculars if any look suspiciously large. Just as we're nearing the entrance to the campsite, we encounter other vehicles and something I was not expecting. Three dogs on the loose. They're running on the road, looking like happy, excited dogs that have managed to escape their human prison. We slow to a crawl before stopping abruptly when one of the dogs runs right in front of Vera. A truck coming the other way has stopped too, and a man in a gilet and wellington boots gets out. It looks like he either knows these dogs or knows who does, as he rounds them up, and we continue onto the campsite.

When we pull up, we can still hear the dogs barking away up the road. Fiona, one of the owners of the site, comes to meet us and directs us to our pitch. She runs a tiny shop on the site, so we buy some milk and a couple of small cakes for later.

I love this place. It feels like we're nestled in a little valley, with hills all around. The site is in a deer conservation area, and when we look up at the hillsides in front and to the side of the van, we see deer with their heads down, quietly grazing. The weather has cleared, and we're pleased to have stopped for the day. We're positioned next to a gently babbling stream, which I believe to be one of the most peaceful sounds you could ever listen to. I often listen to recordings of flowing water when I feel anxious.

I'm happy.

For dinner, we use up the pasta and pasta sauce we brought with us. As we're on our last few days, we should really try to use up what's left in our food bag. James has cooked most evenings, so I'm more than happy to take the reins tonight. I put some water on to boil and then spot something out of the corner of my eye. A gigantic chicken.

No – two gigantic, honey-coloured chickens. They come trotting over and almost hop right into the van, where James is laughing at the sight. I've never cooked with livestock pecking around my feet before. Another one, a smaller hen, arrives. It's a party! I take a short video on my phone while keeping one eye on the pot of bubbling water. After a while, they must sense that it's time to get back to their own home because they slowly waddle away as I'm serving up our supper.

I write some more in my journal before we make up the bed, and James sets his phone to alert us for any aurora borealis activity. It's a gorgeous, clear night. One more chance. We roll down the blinds and snuggle up. It's a cooler night, so we add the weighted blanket. I don't think I've ever felt quite so un-anxious.

16

DAY 12 – A RETURN TO CITY LIFE

It's a bitter-sweet feeling waking up this morning. When I roll up the blinds to let the light in, it's a beautiful day and we're in a beautiful place. Yet, I'm aware that we've also just had our last night in Scotland in the campervan. Today we're heading to Edinburgh, where we'll stop in a hotel for a couple of nights and explore the city. Thankfully, there are no scheduled stops on the way, so we can afford to have a slower morning.

While we sip our tea, made, as usual, by James while I was still dozing, we discuss the day's plans. We want to join a memorial service on Zoom in the afternoon, so we agree to stop before the scheduled start time and join on my phone from the van. We can't check in at our hotel in Edinburgh until 3 pm, so there's no real rush. We'll take it steadily and stop for lunch when we find somewhere nice.

My hair really needs washing today, so while James packs up the kettle and cups, I lug my towel, my wash bag and a change of clothes to the shower. It's a small cubicle but very clean, and the water is hot – but not too hot, thankfully. I've still not shaved my legs and have no intention to. I'm not even sure where my razor is anymore… it's not in my wash bag. Maybe it's in my rucksack.

After awkwardly dressing myself in the tiny space, I exit the cubicle and walk to the other side of the room, where a wall of sinks and mirrors face me. I start my usual hair routine – flip it upside down, finger brush it all out, rake gel through, scrunch and then start the long process of diffusing. However, I don't have my hairdryer with its diffuser attachment, so I briefly use the wall-mounted dryer to hover over it.

I jump when I hear the door to the block open – we're clearly the only ones on the site – only to find that it's James, wanting to check up on me. I've taken so long to get ready, that he was starting to worry that I'd passed out in the hot shower. Happy to know I'm fine and well, just the owner of a lot of hair that won't dry, he returns to the van. Eventually, with a frizzy but clean head of hair, I gather my things and exit the building, flip-flopping my way around the brick walls and along the path the travels through the middle of the camping pitches.

I realise as I walk towards James and Vera that today is the 12th of May, it's the 12th day of our Scotland trip and we're on pitch 12. This happy coincidence feels like a wonderful way to end this stretch of the journey. With the hills behind us and the sun shining, it seems the perfect opportunity to set up a photo of the two of us in the back of the van. I prop my phone on a tree stump while James turns the car around. Five, four, three, two, one…

Flash!

We wave goodbye to Glengoulandie, and I leave a positive review on Google as we trundle down the road. It's around 11 am when we leave, so we drive for an hour or so before stopping to pick up some lunch. During this time, I start to feel quite dizzy. At certain turns of the head, it feels like I'm gradually leaning over to one side even though I'm well aware that I'm stationary. I try to look straight ahead and avoid any sudden movements. This is particularly tricky on single-track country lanes in need of some repairs. Thankfully, the route begins to smooth the closer we get to the city. At lunchtime, we pass a gorgeous village called Dunkeld, where we park. I hold on to James as we walk down the shop- and café-lined street, until we enter a beautiful Scandi-style shop that also sells food. We order toasties. A pesto and mozzarella one for me, and a chicken, pesto and mozzarella one for James. As we sit and wait, the dizziness returns, and it's making me feel a little unwell. James hands me the keys to the van, and I leave him to collect the food and meet me back at the van. I keep my eyes straight ahead as I make my way back down the busy street, trying to put one foot in front of the other in a straight line, until I unlock the door and flop onto the passenger's seat. I close my eyes. Just ten seconds later, James knocks on the window of the driver's door and I let him in.

I really want to enjoy my lunch, but I'm still feeling uneasy. James takes my hand and prays over our lunch, asking that, if possible, I feel better quickly. After slowly eating as much as I can, we get on our way again.

While continuing our drive south, I receive a FaceTime from Laura. She's in Fowey, Cornwall, and has just stepped foot in the house they're staying in. Every year, she and Alex visit the same house in Fowey with

Alex's Mom and Dad. We went with them last year and were invited again this year but sadly couldn't afford to do – or logistically accomplish – both Scotland and Cornwall in the same month.

Laura shows me some upgrades to the house that the owner has made since last year, and we have a little catch-up. She's sad that we're not there with them but happy that we're having such an enjoyable time. We promise to meet up in person as soon as we're both back from our respective holidays, and we say goodbye.

At 2:30 pm, we stop at a service station en route to use the bathroom and log in to the memorial service on Zoom. It's for a couple who were in a tragic car accident. The husband is the brother of my cousin's husband; a loose connection, but James and I met them a handful of times, and it's incredibly sad to have lost them in such a way. The service is being held in London, in a large assembly hall, and we're expecting to see many connections via Zoom.

What we weren't expecting was to not be able to get on at all. When I log in, I receive a message to say that the meeting has reached a maximum of 1,000 participants and to try again later. We attempt to join repeatedly from around 2:40 until 3:00. No joy. I text Mom. She's managed to get in. We connect over FaceTime, and we're able to at least listen to the funeral talk through Mom's phone. It's the most beautiful memorial service. It's warm, sentimental, humorous at times, encouraging. A perfect tribute to two wonderful human beings.

We finally enter Edinburgh and are faced with something we've not really encountered for almost two weeks – traffic. It takes a while to get to the car park we're aiming for, and when we do, we see a potential problem. The car park has one of those barriers on the entrance that prevents vehicles over a certain height from passing through. James gingerly edges towards the barrier but can't make out if we're going to get through. I hop out and assess the situation. The bar is on hinges, so, in theory, it might allow the roof box through, albeit with some minor scratches on the top. While standing by the side of the van, trying to communicate with James, I hear a voice behind me.

'I wouldn't park here if I were you.'

I spin around to see a woman in her forties accompanied by a toddler and pushchair, pointing at the van. I'm worried that this Scottish lady is going to berate us — we look like the stereotypical campervanners-with-a-roof-box-type tourists... I guess that's what we are, really. Instead, I'm pleasantly surprised by the friendly advice she presents.

'The roof in the car park gets super low — even lower than that barrier,' she advises while trying to keep hold of her wandering toddler, 'so I'd try somewhere else.'

'Oh, thank you, that's very helpful,' I awkwardly respond.

'There's another car park just down the road if you go down that way,' she says, pointing past me down the road we came in on, 'then take a right...'

I don't hear much after this. I nod along and express my appreciation for her help before she turns and leaves with her toddler in hand. I turn to James, who's looking at me expectantly. 'She said to try somewhere else; apparently, the roof gets really low, so we might not get out again even if we get in.'

By this time, we're both getting tired, and I haven't got a clue where the local lady said we should try to park, so James makes the executive decision to just go for it. He inches the van through the barrier, which barely makes it through without a scrape, and he pulls into one of the bays in the outdoor part of the car park. We can always take the roof box off before we leave if it doesn't look like it's going to allow us an easy exit. The car park is directly below one side of the famous Edinburgh Castle, so we take a few minutes to sit and look at the tiny people we see on the castle wall.

After catching our breath, we gather our essentials from the van and walk 10 minutes to our hotel. It's lovely. The room is large, clean and complete with a full kitchen. It's also quite warm, so we open the window (as much as it will go) and plonk our stuff down. We collapse on the bed for a few minutes and talk about the funeral. I realise that lying horizontally makes the dizziness worse, so I prop myself up with the sumptuous hotel pillows while we discuss what we're going to do for dinner. There are so many cool, interesting and independent eateries in Edinburgh, but we're both feeling exhausted and can't face the inevitably long decision-making process of choosing where to go. We choose somewhere we know. Zizzi.

It works out perfectly. I'm starting to feel better by the time we stroll around the corner to the restaurant, which is surprisingly quiet for nearing 6 pm on a Friday evening. I'd presumed it would be busy, so I've got my Loop earplugs in to reduce background noise, but I eventually take them out. We eat lots of pasta and pizza, drink, pay up and slowly wander back to the hotel, enjoying the cool evening breeze and watching as young people start to appear, dressed for a night on the town.

Back at the hotel, we sign into our Amazon Prime account on the smart TV in our room and watch a couple of episodes of The Office while settling down for the night. Soon, the lights are off and we're slowly but surely drifting off to sleep.

CLA-CLANK

...

CLA-CLANK

...

CLA-CLANK

A loose manhole cover in the road, directly below our open bedroom window. Despite it now being past midnight, it's a well-used road, so every half a minute or so, the not-exactly-sleep-inducing sound of CLA-CLANK sends a jolt through us both. I'm aware of the noise but can't tell if James is asleep or being kept awake by the disturbance like me. I try to block out the noise. Just as I feel myself drifting off again... CLA-CLANK.

By around 1 am, I can tell that James is still awake too. He's tossing and turning, but he's also pulling the covers off, which tells me that it's not just the noise from the road that's troubling him. I turn to face him, which brings some dizziness back, but I ignore it.

'Are you ok?'

'Not really.'

'Is it that ridiculous drain cover? It's keeping me up too.'

'Yes. But I feel really anxious,' James whispers, 'and a bit sick too.'

What follows is an incredibly long, sleep-deprived night in which I try to calm my husband and avoid having a panic attack myself as a result of seeing him fight a panic attack, all while that infernal drain cover CLA-CLANKs every few seconds. We can't have another night like this. In the morning, we'll ask to move to a room on the other side of the building. Between us, we manage a few hours' sleep before the light coming through the curtains tells us that a new day is starting.

17

DAY 13 – AN ASSAULT ON THE SENSES

After that long, sleepless, warm night, we're both feeling a little rough. James is the first to get up and shower, while I slowly tear myself away from the comfy hotel pillows. We can't have another night like that one, so James heads downstairs to request a room change. By the time I've showered, dressed and got my curly hair to behave, he's back with the news that we've been given a new room for tonight, on the other side of the building. Yay!

We can't move our stuff in there right away, as it's currently occupied, but the reception staff have said that we can put our bags and coats in storage until it's available. The clothes bag feels heavier than I expected, but then I remember that we've not actually had to do much carrying of our bags for the last two weeks. The holdall, especially, has simply sat behind the driver's seat in the van, nestled between the door and our bag of food, for almost two weeks, and all we've needed to do is reach in and pull out fresh clothes as needed.

So, exercising muscles I've not really used for a while, we lug our belongings out the door, down the swelteringly hot hallway, into the lift and out into the reception area, where a young female employee impressively takes them all from us and hands us a luggage tag.

This chain of hotels very handily provides a free breakfast bag for its patrons, which we collect and eat in the seating area by reception. The walls are sage green, the seats are olive green and I've decided to wear a forest green T-shirt. James takes a photo of me, blending in with the décor, sipping my carton of apple juice. We eat our pots of yoghurt and granola and blueberry muffins. James orders extra toast – how he never puts weight on is beyond me.

After finishing breakfast, we head out of the hotel to have a wander around the beautiful city that is Edinburgh. Our hotel is situated a little out of the main hub of the new town sector of the city, so it's a nice, quiet road we find ourselves on as we leave the building.

I always like to check out the local art galleries whenever we're away, and Edinburgh has some excellent opportunities to see famous artworks. The nearest to the hotel is the Scottish National Portrait Gallery. It's about a 15-minute walk down the road, so we get going.

I know you should never completely trust a weather report, but we had been reassured by multiple weather apps that today was going to be a warm one, so I didn't even bother to bring a cardigan. About five minutes into the walk, we look at each other and know we're both thinking the same thing. James is the first to break the silence.

'…Bit chilly, isn't it?'

We laugh and agree that we can't be bothered to turn around to collect more clothing.

'We'll be in and out of shops and galleries all day,' I rationalise, 'so I don't think we'll get too cold. We'd only end up packing jumpers into our bags all day.'

We continue on our route toward the portrait gallery, stepping through pockets of sunshine and shade. There's a green area to the left of us, protected by iron fencing and padlocked gates.

Near the end of the road, we finally arrive at the stone steps leading into the gallery. I'm grateful to be out of the chilly air. It's a beautiful building, and an auburn-bobbed female member of staff welcomes us inside and gives us an overview of the building layout. As soon as we move into the main building, I've forgotten what she said. Thankfully, James has the skill of being able to both listen to someone speaking and then retain that information. I follow his lead as we make our way up the winding stairs.

Passing white plinths topped by marble busts of men I've never heard of, we eventually find ourselves on the first floor, which opens onto a square room with a balcony around the permitter, overlooking the ground floor through a large hole in the middle. An ornate railing forms a protective barrier to prevent us from tumbling back down to ground level. The roof is supported by multiple stone pillars, and the walls feature tapestries and old-looking oil paintings from floor to ceiling.

Meandering through the rooms, several artworks and sculptures interest us, including a blue crystal glass racing helmet, designed in collaboration with Susie Wolff. As avid fans of Formula 1, we're pleasantly surprised to stumble across this work.

Another work that I knew would be here is a painting of renowned violinist Nicola Benedetti. I find it on a large pale wall. It's a huge piece, with much of it in dark tones to highlight the lemon-yellow light pouring in from a stained glass window in Westminster Abbey. The other-worldly light bathes the musician, creating an ethereal feel. I like it.

Towards the exit of the gallery, I spy another painting I've seen on TV as well. Samira Addo painted Emili Sande in the final of Portrait Artist of the Year in 2018, which she went on to win. The purple tones and yellow highlights of the hair stand out against the red brick wall on which the artwork sits.

Knowing that we're not rushing to drive to another campsite today is a lovely feeling. We gradually make our way through the gift shop, escaping – amazingly – with our money intact, and take a gentle stroll toward the royal mile.

As a word of warning for anyone who struggles with loud noises or busy crowds, I suggest avoiding this section of Edinburgh on a hot Saturday afternoon. Near the bottom of the hill, it's busy, but not overwhelming, and I can enjoy people watching and window shopping as we amble toward the castle at the top. However, with every few metres we advance, the crowds grow, and before long, it's difficult to make our way through. Musicians in kilts line the sides of the street here and there, with bagpipes just about breaking through the chatter of the masses charging through. One is a child, about 10 years old, who has drawn in a large audience.

In time, we make it to the entrance to the castle. We're quite happy to save our pennies and just enjoy the view from this side of the castle rather than join the hundreds on the other side. We find a gap in a row of people and lean on the pointed wall, looking over the Old Town area. We hear many accents, but mostly American. The sky is blue, with the occasional streak of a wispy cloud. There is a line of buses below, likely picking up and dropping off holidaymakers and tourists who want to see the famous castle. A large brick building that looks like a former factory looms over the roofs of other houses and shops. Behind it are the shadows of mountains and hills.

It's nearing lunchtime, so we leave the castle grounds to hunt for food. Walking down the steep roads that lead away from the Royal Mile, we pass beautiful stone houses with brightly coloured doors and black metal fencing. I take a photo. I plan to draw them later.

Almost every café or restaurant we walk by is overflowing. Our feet are starting to ache from all the walking, and I really fancy a cup of tea. Think, Rosie. Where might not be too busy? Then it hits me – you can always count on an art gallery to have a café. And since not everyone is interested in art, there are usually seats available. The National, formerly the Scottish National Gallery, is just five minutes' walk away. After strolling to the wrong side of the building to begin with, we finally find the entrance to the café, which has outside seating too. A two-seat table awaits us. Its parasol shields us from the afternoon sun. We get a pot of tea. I have soup.

In the orange-tinged light caused by the parasol, James looks incredibly tanned. I chuckle and take a photo.

After lunch, I ask James if he'd mind if we took a wander around the gallery itself, while we're here. I've seen on a sign that there's a van Gogh on show, so I'm eager to have a look. When we enter, we see signs that point upstairs for van Gogh and other artists. Heading to the stairway, though, a barrier blocks our way. A sign reveals that there are works being undertaken, apparently. Shame. Almost perfect.

Still, there are many works of art that we can access, one of them being Landseer's Monarch of the Glen, which is, simply put, amazing. It feels imposing, sat high on the wall, as though the stag is really standing on a tall grassy ridge on the other side of the partition. It's nice and quiet inside the gallery. Art seems to attract interesting, sometimes unusual characters, yet they're all generally polite and subdued people.

The gift shop is cool – in both senses of the word – so we take advantage of the air conditioning and peruse the expensive souvenirs. I pick up a sketchbook that makes me laugh. The cover says, 'MY ARTWORK IS TERRIBLE AND I AM A VERY BAD PERSON'. We spy a jigsaw – a classic holiday gift – of an old map of Scotland and get it for Vince and Judith.

After that, we wander through some high-street shops. It feels a bit criminal to be hopping in and out of the shops we'd find at home after two weeks of countryside and independent stores. But we're in Edinburgh now, not a quaint little village. I buy a new pair of Converse from Office. Pastel green – I seem to be buying everything in that colour lately.

In one of the small parks, we buy iced coffees from a stall and sit in the dappled shade of a tree. Lots of people pass by. A patient mother with two young children stops in front of us to tend to one child who is dragging his feet beside her while her other wriggles around in the pushchair. There is a warm breeze and a gentle hubbub around us, produced by the small groups of people who are also sitting on the grass in this park. It's nearing dinnertime, and we need to decide whether to head back to the hotel to change or simply stay out until finding somewhere to eat. The slow ambling around the city has made us quite tired, and my feet are feeling it. So the option with the least amount of walking feels like the right choice. We gather our belongings and start strolling towards where most of the restaurants are.

Our preference for dinner is Dishoom – an Indian–tapas-inspired restaurant, which Luke and Dani have repeatedly encouraged us to visit. There's one in Birmingham, but we never seemed to have the time or opportunity to eat there. As we approach the front of the building that houses Dishoom, there's already a small queue forming at the entrance. After a good but tiring day of exploring Edinburgh, neither of us particularly fancy a loud, busy restaurant. But we join the queue and ask a member of staff who pops out of the front to invite people inside how busy it is.

'We're pretty packed right now,' he explains, glancing back to the darkly lit interior. 'I can fit you in, but it'll be about a 30-minute wait.'

I look up at James, who doesn't need me to say anything to know what I'm thinking.

'Find somewhere else?'

'I think so,' I answer.

We'll try Dishoom another day when it's a little quieter and we can enjoy it properly. We step out of the queue and take a look around. There are eateries that we've never heard of, but it's always a risk when you've not been somewhere before. Is the food any good? Are the portion sizes tiny? I spy a favourite of ours just down the road. A chain restaurant, but always a winner. Wagamama. Not too adventurous, but good food that we know and love.

There's no queue, and it's not too busy inside. In fact, we find a two-person table on the upper floor that overlooks the level below. We sit next to the railing, peering over the top to see the chefs in the kitchen. One of them is struggling to get rice out of an almond-shaped mould. The other benefit to Wagamama is that there are plenty of vegetarian options. When we go out for dinner, I often only have a handful of meat-free meals to choose from. But here, it's often James waiting for me to choose what I want. We both choose versions of Yaki Soba. A delicious and calm end to a full, noisy day.

Unbeknownst to us, it gets colder outside while we sit enjoying our noodles. When we leave through the front door of the restaurant, James gives me his jacket and braves the cold. We walk briskly back to the hotel, grateful to step through the entry doors to a warm reception area. Thankfully, our new room is ready, so we collect a key card and our bags from the storage area and take the lift up to the fourth floor. Leaving the lift, the corridor is still swelteringly warm. Why are all hotel corridors the same? Finally, we find our door number and let ourselves in. The room has the same décor and design of our original room but is a little smaller.

However, it is quieter and feels cosier, so it's all good in our books.

Exhausted, we peel our shoes off and flop onto the bed. I switch the huge wall-mounted TV on and watch some of Eurovision. James doesn't like the craziness of the show, so he takes out his iPad and catches up on MasterChef. Eurovision does get madder every year. I still find the whole event entertaining, but some of the performances even I have to mute. Nan would have hated it.

The programme will be on for a long time, but my eyelids feel heavy. The lack of sleep last night and the thousands of steps covered today are catching up with us now. James has slowly sunk under the covers and is beginning to close his eyes. Before I lose the motivation, I get changed into my pyjamas and get ready for bed. iPad and TV off, I stop and listen for minute or so. No clanking drain covers yet....

18

DAY 14 – ENDINGS

I open my eyes, and I'm confused to see light peering around the edges of the closed curtains. However, I'm quickly delighted to realise that it's morning and I've had a full night's sleep. I turn to James, who is on his phone. I'm worried he's not slept well again, but thankfully he's just been awake for a while and slept well too. Since today is our last in Scotland, I'm glad for a good start to the day. But we're out of milk. I can't remember the last time we didn't start a morning with a cup of tea, so to rectify this terrifying prospect, James gets dressed and pops downstairs to ask for some milk. While he's there, he gets two paper bags of breakfast and brings them back up to the room. Soon, we're sipping tea and discussing the day ahead.

We'll be leaving for the Lake District this afternoon, but we want to savour the last few hours in Scotland. Fourteen amazing days. When I think back to Ardfern and that tick bite that freaked me out so much, it feels like years ago. The routine of packing up, travelling on, settling down for the night and then starting again the next day had become so normal, even in just two weeks, that staying two nights in one hotel in Edinburgh seemed wrong. But it's been lovely to stop and breathe for a couple of days before making our way back home.

We pack our bags and get ready for our final Scottish day before heading downstairs to hand in our key and make our way back to Vera. I'm wearing my new pair of Converse, of course – who doesn't immediately wear a new item of clothing after they've bought it? But after 10 minutes of brisk walking to the car, I'm regretting my decision. I can feel the blisters growing on the back of my heels, and the weight of the bags I'm carrying isn't helping. I make eye contact with James, who can see a vague grimace on my face and laughs.

'The shoes?' He asks.

I wince and nod. Should have worn them in a bit first. The knowledge that I'll be able to apply some plasters once we get to the car keeps me moving. Every few steps, I transfer the weight of the bag onto my other arm. Finally reaching Vera, James loads our bags inside while I carefully unwrap and apply plasters to my shiny, puffy, red heels. We're heading into Edinburgh's Old Town this morning, which I hope will be somewhat quieter than what we experienced yesterday. From the car park, we take some steep concrete steps down to the road that leads up to the base of the castle mount, which we circle, peering up at the stone walls and tiny heads appearing over their edges. We take a left onto West Bow, a winding street on an incline that's spotted with colourful shop fronts. Multicoloured bunting gently flaps in the breeze above our heads as we venture towards a French-inspired café to buy coffee and pastries. Well, we've got to keep our energy up somehow.

Before we stop to eat, we run into the Skye Candle Co. shop next door, where a tall, stocky, loud man greets us from behind the counter. Within 30 seconds, he's sworn more than I think we've heard anyone swear in the two weeks we've been away. I politely edge away, trying to sidestep into a small room off the main shop floor that houses lots of cute cards as well as candles in tins of various shades. I'm not really a talker when I'm scanning a shop's products; I'm quite happy to peruse in my own world. But this man, as friendly and upbeat as he is, doesn't seem to pick up on the vibes. Thankfully, James keeps him occupied while I choose a candle in a dark-green–labelled tin, which will fit right in with our bathroom's colour scheme at home. I make polite chit-chat while I pay, eager to get out of the loud man's shop. As soon as we step out of the front, James and I exchange glances and laugh as we walk away.

Although it's an overcast day, it's bright and dry, so we decide to eat outside to try to take in the city while we're here. We find a set of stone steps leading down to the New Town and park ourselves on the top one. People have attached padlocks to the fencing all the way from the top step to the bottom, even though this isn't a famous flight of steps or even a central one. Some are engraved, while others are inscribed with a Sharpie pen. A 'Sabrina & Mark' attached theirs on 20th November 2008. I wonder what they're up to now.

An older man with a road bike in tow ascends the many steps in front of us. He takes a breath at the top, and we both smile at him.

'Are you local?' James asks. I've always struggled with being conversational with people I don't know, but James seems to have the knack for striking up conversations.

'No,' the balding man says, breathlessly. 'I'm currently cycling to Thurso – I've been all around France, and now I'm heading home.'

'We were in Thurso for a bit,' James explains, and the two briefly exchange experiences of travelling.

As we watch him walk away with his bike, a couple stride towards us, carrying some luggage. In posh accents, they ask us where the steps lead, and James hazards a guess but explains that we're only visiting and that we don't know the area too well. They seem satisfied with our guestimate but frown as they look at the number of steps to navigate.

'Do you think we'll get down in one trip?' The lady asks her husband. I reckon they're in their late sixties, and I'm about to offer help when James stands and offers to carry a bag or two. I love this man.

They were clearly hoping for such an offer because they're only too happy to accept, with the white-haired man holding up a large holdall for James to take. I watch as James and the posh couple clamber down the steps and around the bend, disappearing from view. A moment later, James reappears and runs back up again, almost making it to the top without stopping.

'More steps than I thought,' he says, breathlessly. I smile and brush the croissant crumbs from my jeans before standing to join him.

'Shall we?'

'I guess so,' James says, after getting his breath back and taking one last look over the cityscape before us.

We wander our way to the car, conscious that the roof box is still very much on top of the van, which could be an issue when it comes to exiting the car park. I push the worry out of my mind as I listen to the growing hubbub and take mental snapshots of the old buildings we pass.

To leave the car park, we need to go below ground and out the other side of the road. The ceiling in the underground section is low. As we edge the van further into the underground car park, it's not clear if we'll get through without scraping the roof box on some of the low-hanging concrete beams and lights. I jump out and take a few steps back. James rolls down his window.

'Keep going,' I shout. 'But slowly.'

Over a few minutes, James takes a slow, tentative drive through the car park, with me walking at a distance beside the van, pausing to check the distance between the top of the roof box and the bottom of the ceiling. Barely a centimetre saves the roof box at some stages. But, finally, we make it to the exit barrier unscathed. Next stop, The Lakes.

Our last stay before we see our Gordon again is Pound Farm in Kendal. It's a site James visited many times as a child with his family, of which he has fond memories, and it feels a fitting way to end the trip. It's three hours away, and we watch as the scenery changes before us. On the way, we stop at a Morrisons to pick up some provisions for tonight's dinner, and I find a dinosaur-shaped plant pot, which I immediately decide to buy for our friend Andy, Jo's husband. It can be his father-to-be present.

When we eventually pull into the driveway after the lengthy journey, we trundle through the middle of the site. Brown wooden caravans sit haphazardly in the patches of field on either side of the track, which eventually opens onto a grassy patch with gravel rectangles spaced out for a dozen vehicles. There's a small incline in one corner, forming a little knoll. James remembers this 'hill' but finds that it is much smaller than he remembers. He is, however, a foot taller now than he was back then.

Parking the van into a bay and doing our best to make it level with chocks under the front tyres, we take a walk around to check out the facilities. We've been spoilt with most of the sites we've stayed on, with clean, light, airy showers and toilets. When I step into the ladies WC, it's damp and dark, with spiders keeping a close eye on me from every corner. I laugh to myself. What a fine end to a fantastic trip. I tip-toe across the moist floor and look in the murky mirror. I don't see Nan in my round face; sadly I haven't inherited any of her features (or height). I wish I could give her a call and tell her all about these two weeks. She'd have loved a catch-up.

In the months before she died, Nan struggled to speak, which made it difficult to converse. But she always had a happy face whenever family popped in. I remember a few weeks before her final day, my cousins Lynne and Penny visited Nan, as she'd taken a turn for the worse. I met them there, and when I stepped into the room, Nan gave me the biggest smile and weakly, but brightly, voiced, 'Hello!'. My cousins joked about me being the favourite granddaughter. I miss that smile.

It's late afternoon and the sun is starting to disappear behind the trees, with a peachy hue taking over the sky. There isn't much in the way of a view at this campsite, but opposite the entrance is a large field, so before settling down for our last night away, James and I walk together between the brown caravans down the dusty path toward the entryway. As we turn to head straight for the end of the path, the golden light catches us by surprise. The green fields beyond the opposite wall have olive, khaki and jade tones as the light seeps over the low hills. We stand for a few minutes and watch as the sheep, scattered around the area, begin to meander in the same direction, likely heading to their home for the night. And, as we turn and walk back to Vera, so do we.

The evening is a relaxed and reflective one. James makes dinner – veggie sausage and squash stew – while I set up a final game of Scrabble. We realise that we haven't quite balanced the car evenly, so we have to sleep with our heads at the door-end of the van. Why hadn't we thought of this sooner? We're able to prop ourselves up against the doors rather than awkwardly fold the bed slats into an upright position. We laugh at yet another 'almost perfect' moment, thinking of all the mornings and evenings when we could have saved time and prevented overstretching our arms just from repositioning the bed. We know for next time. Tomorrow we head home. We'll pick up Gordon and have a cup of tea at Mom's before returning to the flat. How soon we'll be back to reality.

As we roll down the blinds on each window to darken the interior of the van, we discuss our favourite moments from the past 14 days. So many highlights come to mind – the campsite at Skye, climbing the Old Man of Storr, the beaches at Durness – but the standout point for me was standing in the fog outside a closed museum in Wick, surrounded by topsy-turvy gravestones, holding up a photograph of my wonderful Nan. James puts his arm around me as I take a moment to remember her and think of all the things I've got to tell her when I see her again. Then it will be me beaming at her, saying, 'Hello, Nan.'

ACKNOWLEDGEMENTS

I have to start by thanking my supportive, encouraging and stupendously patient husband, James. From reading my very first journal entries in Scotland to the final draft of this book, he has given me the nudges I needed to not give up. Thank you. I love you.

Without talking to Auntie Hazel, Nan's beloved sister, I wouldn't have known about some of the details of their trip to Scotland that enthused me to write about them. Thank you for being a great sister to my Nan.

Mom, your insistence that I should finish this book and your genuine confidence that I could do a good job has been touching and uplifting. Thank you for looking after Nan and me.

Thank you, Dad, for gifting me your Irish determination, which helped me to keep writing.

To my cousin Penny, thank you for being a fellow book nerd and for cheering me on and giving me invaluable suggestions. I won't be offended if you don't give me five stars on Goodreads.

I am blessed to have wonderful in laws, including a father-in-law and mother-in-law, Vince and Judith, who have never failed to make me feel at home. Thank you for camping with us, lending us tools and always being there for James and me. Laura and Alex, my sister-in-law and brother-in-law, thank you for taking us on holiday with you and bearing with me when I struggle up the slightest of inclines. Luke and Dani, my brother-in-law and sister-in-law, thank you for the anniversary present, *Take the Slow Road – Scotland*, which inspired many of the routes we took on this trip.

Auntie Davina was instrumental in making our campervan comfortable; thank you for lending us your superb sewing skills. And thank you, Auntie Rachel, for gifting us the fabric for our sofa cushions.

To Uncle Steve and Auntie Barbara and Caleb and Izzy, thank you for camping with us as we prepared our little campervan for the trip. We loved spending time with you.

ABOUT THE AUTHOR

Rosie Clifton was born in Birmingham, UK. She works as a proofreader and editor from her home – still in Birmingham – usually with Gordon the cat curled up on her lap.

Tea on the Way North is her first book.

Printed in Great Britain
by Amazon

62510635R00099